A TREASURY OF ICONS

A TREASURY

Kurt Weitzmann

Manolis Chatzidakis

Krsto Miatev

and Svetozar Radojčić

OF ICONS

SIXTH TO SEVENTEENTH CENTURIES

FROM THE SINAI PENINSULA, GREECE, BULGARIA, AND YUGOSLAVIA

HARRY N. ABRAMS, INC., NEW YORK

ORIGINAL TITLE: IKONE SA BALKANA
TRANSLATED BY ROBERT ERICH WOLF
LIBRARY OF CONGRESS CATALOG CARD NUMBER: 67-12687
COPYRIGHT 1966 IN YUGOSLAVIA BY "JUGOSLAVIJA," BELGRADE,
"BLGARSKI HUDOŽNIK," SOFIA

CONTENTS

INTRODUCTORY NOTE

The icons reproduced in this book are published together for the first time, and have been selected from the collections of churches and museums in three Balkan countries: Greece, Bulgaria, and Yugoslavia. They represent the great wealth of icon painting that the Balkans have created and preserved through the centuries. To this material have been added the early icons found in the Monastery of Saint Catherine on the Sinai peninsula and photographed during the Alexandria-Michigan-Princeton archaeological expeditions. But no attempt has been made to present these icons in terms of the national origins of their artists, for this cannot be determined with certainty in many cases. Icons have been transplanted from one country to another throughout their long history. Furthermore, the masters who painted for a particular court or dignitary were often themselves from abroad. Patrons and foreign rulers also endowed churches and monasteries with icons as votive offerings, or as donations for special occasions. Particularly coveted as spoils of war, icons were constantly transported from one country to another. Even when they remained in the region of their origin, subsequent political changes affected the boundaries of most of the nations to which the anonymous artists had belonged. Thus, the icons found within the present frontiers of the Balkan countries cannot be ascribed to any one country in particular, and an attempt to study icons according to their national origins would inevitably meet so many difficulties that the finest examples of Balkan art would often have to be omitted. That is why this book is organized according to the present-day frontiers of the countries in which the icons are found, rather than according to the countries within which the icons were made.

This plan makes it possible to complete the diversified panorama of the wealth of icons that have survived in these countries. It also helps us to trace the two parallel developments of the icon, as a religious object and as a cultural phenomenon. Only thus can one get a rounded presentation of the iconography — the pictorial symbols and conventions of these works — which for so many centuries fulfilled the religious and aesthetic needs of the Orthodox peoples of the eastern Mediterranean basin. Exceptions to this plan of regional organization have been made in the chapter on Greece, in order that certain icons now in Istanbul, Jerusalem, Cyprus, and southern Italy might be included; the chapter on Yugoslavia also discusses icons that are now in Ravenna and in the Monastery of Chilandar on Mount Athos.

Four world-famous specialists here set forth their views and support them convincingly. All future investigations in this field will inevitably owe much to these contributions to the understanding of the art of the icon.

I. SINAI PENINSULA

Icon Painting from the Sixth to the Twelfth Century *by Kurt Weitzmann*

Plates 1—36

From the writings of the early Fathers of the Church it appears that the type of picture we call an icon only very gradually took on the specific meaning that the Orthodox Church attributed to it during and after the Iconoclast movement. The way for its veneration was prepared by that of relics, and especially of those of the Holy Cross, in the fourth century. But it is not until the fifth century that we find the cult of holy images mentioned by Augustine, Epiphanius of Salamis, and others, and not until the first half of the sixth century that there is a reference, by Hypatius of Ephesus, to a proskynesis, an act of prostration before an icon. By a half-century later, in the period following the reign of Justinian, accounts of icons and their miraculous powers became more numerous. From then on, though iconoclasts and apologists continued to dispute the question, the veneration of holy images gained ground steadily until 726. It was then that the Iconoclast movement, which objected to any kind of depiction of the Divine, put a temporary halt to any further development.[1] Between the sixth and early eighth centuries there was a change from the old concept of the icon as no more than a religious object of immediate utility, to a new attitude of greater spirituality stressing the transcendental relationship between the image and the holy personage depicted. This provided the basis for the clear formulations concerning the significance of icons which were finally made by John of Damascus and Theodore the Studite.

Until recently only four icons of any importance were known from this earliest phase. These were icons from the Monastery of Saint Catherine on Mount Sinai, which were brought to Kiev by the Russian archimandrite Porphyrius Uspensky in the middle of the nineteenth century.[2] But a few years ago our knowledge was significantly increased when George and Maria Sotiriou made known further material from the pre-Iconoclast period which had survived in Saint Catherine's monastery.[3] Among those icons are two of such outstanding quality that we are inclined to attribute them to one of the workshops in Constantinople, although all attempts made so far to localize and date these and other early icons must be considered hypothetical.

One of the icons depicts the Virgin enthroned with the Child and flanked, as if by two pylons, 1, 2, 3 by the warrior-saints Theodore and George. In a second picture plane, two angels gaze up toward the hand of God from which a ray of light streams down upon the head of Mary. In contrast to the stiff frontal poses of the two saints, who are dressed in the garments of the Imperial bodyguard, the artist permitted the Virgin a limited freedom of movement, turning her eyes to the right and her knees to the left. This freedom is accentuated in the diagonal pose of the Christ Child whose legs are drawn up in typical baby fashion, although the head is that of an adult with emphasis on the high forehead to bring out the spirituality and divinity He represents. From the artistic standpoint, it is above all in the heads that expressive power is concentrated. The dark olive-colored shadows on Mary's face underline her remoteness from reality, her divinity; in contrast, the sun-tanned face of Theodore and the pallor of the youthful George are more true to life. Moreover, the thicker and broader use of paint for the angels' heads, which are still very much in the antique tradition, is an attempt to convey pictorially the ethereal quality of such creatures of Heaven and represents a third mode of expression. In view of the soft, well-modeled plastic treatment of the figures, we are inclined to date this icon as early as the sixth century, although others opt for a century later. In either case, it goes back to a period in which the icon style proper had only just begun to crystallize.

The generally accepted notion that religious cult in classical antiquity found its essential expression in statues of its gods while Christianity adopted the painted image by preference is true only in part. Antiquity was not unacquainted with painted images of the gods, as is known from certain panels depicting enthroned gods which have been found in Fayum;[4] a few painted wings from triptychs also show gods standing upright, and these presumably once flanked central panels of other gods seated on thrones.[5] Although the diffusion of this form of panel painting in antiquity and its influence on Christian art cannot be demonstrated in detail, the examples quoted above are proof that there was a pagan antecedent for both the form and the content of icons.

5   Our second masterpiece of early icon painting[6] is an almost life-size half-figure of Saint Peter with the cross-staff in one hand and a bundle of keys in the other. His penetrating gaze squarely meets the viewer, while his inner emotion, expressed pictorially by the sweep of his hair and his slightly curved beard, is counteracted by the firm grip of his hands, creating an impression of concentrated energy. The three medallion busts above the niche, which in itself serves to give the picture a solid structure, include Christ in the central position, turned slightly toward one side, and the Virgin and a youthful saint (most probably John the Evangelist) on either side. The versatile artist applied here the same principle as that used by the painter of the icon of the Virgin: a somewhat animated central figure placed between two immobile figures. Closely associated with this is the use of an abstract style for the flanking medallion busts. These, in fact, are reminiscent of certain portraits in encaustic from the Fayum.[7] Their abstract style contrasts with the more naturalistic one which goes back to an older classical tradition merely suggested in the head of Christ but brought out fully in the head of Saint Peter. Further evidence of this link with antique painting is the impressionistic technique used for the draperies of Peter. On the other hand, the highlights are already subjected to a process of ornamental stylization which was to become the rule in the later development of Byzantine painting. This in itself suggests a later date for this icon than that of the Virgin, possibly already the seventh century.

Portrait icons also have their roots in pre-Christian art, notably in the official portrait of the emperor, the "lauraton." Even after Christianity had become the state religion, this form continued to be venerated for some time. The sixth-century historian Malalas tells us that the imperial portrait of Constantine the Great was still carried about in processions and worshiped by the current emperor.[8] A panel painting, now in Berlin, of the portraits of Septimius Severus and his family appears to be such a "lauraton."[9] It is in the form of a disc, and this form also survived for a long time in icons.[10] In the icon of Saint Peter under discussion, the arrangement of the three medallions is an obvious parallel to that of the Emperor and Empress, and the Second Consul found on certain ivory consular diptychs.[11] This makes it clear that there was a direct link between icons and imperial images.

Besides those pictorial types derived from the worship of gods and emperors, icon painting at an early period developed others that were new creations of Christian art, especially narrative 8, 9   scenes from the Old and New Testaments. A characteristic example is the icon of the Three Hebrews in the Fiery Furnace. Like the two icons already discussed, this one was done in encaustic, a technique familiar to us from Egyptian mummy portraits. As far as this limited material permits any general conclusions, it may be said that encaustic was the principal, though

X

not the only, medium used for icons in the pre-iconoclastic period, and that it was discontinued in the post-iconoclastic period. Dressed in Persian costume, the three youths stand praying in the midst of a sea of spiral-shaped flames. An angel lays one hand comfortingly on the shoulder of the youth nearest him and in the other he holds, proleptically in this Old Testament scene, a cross-staff signifying that the Hebrew youths would soon be saved by the Cross of Christ.[12] The style here is highly expressive but not as refined as in the icons discussed earlier. The figures are somewhat thickset and have simplified outlines, the highlights are more ornamentalized, and the cloaks are decorated with a pattern of dotted circles. The Sinai collection includes several other icons of the same stylistic trend, for which we propose Palestine as the place of origin;[13] to all intents and purposes, this means Jerusalem — the center with which the Sinai monastery has been most closely connected from earliest times to the present.

In the same stylistic group belongs an icon of the Crucifixion in which Christ, following the *6, 7* Palestinian tradition, is depicted wearing a colobium, a tunic decorated with a pattern similar to that on the mantles of the Three Hebrews in the Fiery Furnace. As is usual, Christ is flanked by Mary[14] and John, and, in addition, by the two thieves, who are here given the apocryphal names of Gestas and Dimas. In terms of iconography this Crucifixion has a special significance; it is, as far as we know now, the earliest example of Christ that shows His eyes closed and the crown of thorns,[15] although highly stylized. These features initiate the development of the type that predominates in the later Middle Ages, the suffering Christ on the Cross.

According to its style, this Crucifixion must be dated a little later than the icon of the Three Hebrews. Comparatively speaking, its closest parallel is to a fresco of the Crucifixion in Santa Maria Antiqua in Rome, which was executed shortly before the middle of the eighth century.[16] Assuming that our icon was also done about the mid-eighth century, then it must stem from the period when icons were banned in the Empire. This, in fact, appears highly probable, for precisely the reason we assumed that it originated in Palestine, a region then under Islamic control and in which the iconoclastic decrees of the Byzantine emperors had no power. It must be remembered that it was in the Monastery of Saint Saba close to Jerusalem that John of Damascus wrote his *Apology in Defense of the Holy Images,* by which means he must certainly have hoped to ensure the continuing production of icons in Palestine. The Monastery of Saint Catherine on Mount Sinai, always dependent on Jerusalem, possesses more icons from this critical period, thus supporting the idea that there was no interruption in the production of icons in that region.

The period after the termination of the iconoclastic controversy has been rightly described as the second Golden Age of Byzantium. In the tenth century, especially, Constantinople produced manuscript illuminations of the highest quality along with works in gold and silver, carved ivory, and cloisonné enamel. The reawakened feeling for antique forms was at times so marked as to justify calling this period the Macedonian Renaissance.[17] But no icons from this flourishing period were known until the recent discovery of a few examples in Sinai. While these do not suffice to fill the deplorable gap in our knowledge of the artistic monuments of that epoch, they do help us to reconstruct the history of icon painting in this important century. The seated figure of the Apostle Thaddeus, which occupies the upper half of a wing of a triptych, bears eloquent *11* testimony to the new renaissance spirit. The new feeling is expressed, among other ways, by the gentle billowing-out of the draperies through which is created a stronger plasticity, although the artist achieves only rarely a convincing impression of a solid body beneath the drapery. Especially striking are the light pastel-like colors,[18] so much like those used in miniature painting at the end of the ninth and the beginning of the tenth century. They recall those of a well-known manuscript, now in the Bibliothèque Nationale in Paris, the Homilies of Gregory of Nazianzus. In fact, our dating of icons of the middle Byzantine period must generally depend on stylistic comparisons with manuscripts, for which dates can more easily be determined.

Yet this relatively more plastic style did not predominate in the tenth century. A rather more dematerialized human body was preferred, especially for depictions of saints, Fathers of the Church, and monks — more in keeping with the ascetic ideal of monasticism. A *13* characteristic example is an icon of Saints Zosimus and Nicholas, although it has in common with the icon of Thaddeus a very free and painterly brush technique, derived ultimately from study of late antique or early Christian models.

In the second half of the tenth century appears a hardening of the painterly style; this goes hand in hand with an often enamel-like brilliance in the treatment of surfaces. It seems very likely that the subtle technique of cloisonné enamel, then at its highest point of development, must have exercised a profound influence on both icon and miniature painting. An icon of the *14, 15* youthful Apostle Philip shows clearly this change of style. Instead of indicating the folds of the drapery by lightly brushed-in highlights in the impressionistic manner, the folds are rendered here by sharp lines. Especially characteristic is the treatment of the folds over the apostle's upper thigh, which imitates the channeled effects of drilled marble in late antique sculpture. This technique, however, was not derived directly from the ancient source but from a particular group of contemporary ivory carvings in which the surfaces are treated in the same way.[19]

The tenth century was a formative period during which iconography and, to a certain extent at least, style itself tended toward standardized conventions. By the end of the century variants were beginning to disappear. Icons for the cycle of the great church feasts became crystallized into forms that can be termed canonical. Depictions of saints were so rigidly characterized that the slightest variation in the treatment of hair or beards was enough to make clear which particular *16* saint was intended. A half-length figure of Saint Nicholas, the most popular of all saints as is shown by the large number of icons devoted to him in the Sinai monastery, still represents the phase before standardization; and for that reason this icon, the earliest of Saint Nicholas known to us, can still be ascribed to the end of the tenth century. The face is treated in a very subtle and painterly manner. Its organic structure is clear and as yet free of the exaggerations — the overly high forehead and the ornamental treatment of hair — which characterize later icons of this saint. On the other hand, what is typical of later development is the series of medallions with busts of saints which decorates the frame and occupies the place that is filled by cloisonné enamels in the more lavish icons of the tenth and eleventh centuries.[20] These small busts already show the tendency toward the precious and miniature-like style which was to become the rule in the eleventh century.

21 The slenderness of the figures on an icon of the Crucifixion strikes us almost as a reaction against *11* the physical solidity of Thaddeus. The figure of Christ, draped in a transparent loincloth, has an organic structure which reveals an understanding of the human body, but the body is at once so elongated as to give the impression of being weightless. John is still depicted with a certain degree of physical reality, convincing mostly through its use of antique-style motifs for the folds of the drapery; while the Virgin is so enveloped in a maphorion that the body beneath it is almost completely hidden. Typical of a great many icons of the eleventh to thirteenth centuries is the effect of a rotating nimbus around the heads, which is achieved by a circular roughening of the gold background. These haloes, imitating a highly refined goldsmith's technique, work together with the brilliant enamel-like surfaces of the painted areas to create an impression of preciousness such as we associate with reliquaries, especially those containing particles of the Holy Cross.

This effect is even stronger in the nimbi around the medallion busts painted on the frame. These are set in a fixed hierarchical order. John the Baptist is in the center, flanked on either side by an archangel, and each archangel has in turn an apostle at one side; then follow various saints, beginning with the Fathers of the Church, as the most important. The hierarchy is that of the liturgical prayer for intercession, and it is an excellent example of how the liturgical element itself dominated the art of the middle Byzantine period, and in particular icon painting. On the central axis, directly beneath the Cross, is the bust of Saint Catherine; this may be taken as a hint that the icon was made for the monastery dedicated to her on Mount Sinai, although it is not necessarily proved that the icon was itself executed there. First of all Constantinople should be taken into consideration as a place that could have produced an icon of such high technical perfection.

The tendency toward refinement in the icon painting of this period often creates an effect of minuteness that is closely related to manuscript illumination — to such an extent that from time to time one has the impression that the icon painter and the miniaturist may have been the same artist. Direct borrowings from the miniature art, not only in technique but also in content, are seen most clearly when the icon painter enters the special province of the miniaturist and adopts its narrative cycles. Excerpts, for example, were made from the lives of saints, and the separate scenes were either arranged around the raised frame of the icon,[21] as was to become the most customary practice, or else painted on the panel itself; in the case of triptychs, these scenes were placed on the wings. Thus, on a panel fragment we find beneath a Virgin of the Annunciation two scenes from the life of Saint Nicholas — his ordination as a priest and, *17* later, a bishop — done in a remarkably delicate miniature-like style, which to all intents and purposes cannot be distinguished from the style in use at the time for manuscript illumination. The fragment is the upper half of a triptych wing, whose lower half, still extant, contains four later scenes from the Saint's life; the lost left-hand wing must have had the Angel of Annunciation along with six more scenes, while still others must have appeared on the lost central panel.

In a similar, miniature-like style that again reveals its origin in manuscript illumination is an icon of the Nativity with many related episodes disposed in such a way that most of the individual *22, 23* scenes maintain the isolation they would have had if they were still intercalated into the columns of text in a Gospel or Lectionary. The icon painter did not line up the individual scenes according to any scheme, but inserted them between overlapping ranges of mountains. These, however, resemble *coulisses*, theatrical scenery, and remain ornamental, with no apparent spatial depth, the latter being a notion which would not have occurred to the painter. The Nativity is presented as taking place in a cave and is framed by scenes illustrating the Annunciation to the Shepherds and the Arrival, Adoration, and Departure of the Magi: these accessory scenes were common in other feast icons of Christmas. To these, however, were here added the Dream of Joseph, the Flight into Egypt (with a welcoming personification of the city), the Concealment of Elisabeth and the young John, and the Massacre of the Innocents. For all of these episodes parallels can easily be found in the extensive cycles of eleventh-century depictions of the Gospel stories,[22] whereas the charming episode of the midwives carrying vessels to the place of the Nativity with which to bathe the newborn Child is a genre scene otherwise unknown to us. The source must have been a manuscript with numerous illustrations of the sacred event.

One cannot avoid the impression that the icon of the Scala Paradisi, the Ladder to Heaven, *19* must have been copied directly from the title-page miniature in one of the many manuscripts of the treatise on that subject by John Climacus.[23] The monks clamber zealously up the thirty rungs of the ladder, corresponding to the thirty virtues treated by John in an equal number of chapters. Their ascent is impeded by the temptations of vices, personified by tiny devils who try to cause the stumbling monks to fall. Only one has virtually succeeded in reaching the goal of Heaven; this is John Climacus himself, the author of the treatise and the abbot of the monastery on Mount Sinai. Directly behind him follows a certain Archbishop Anthony, who most likely was another abbot of Sinai, presumably at the period when the icon was made, which means sometime during the eleventh to twelfth centuries. The quality of this icon as a work of art is revealed in the animated rhythm of the climbing monks, in the mixture of typified and individual characterization in the heads, and, not least, in the subtle color range of the monks' garments. This range is rich in nuances and at the same time subdued, in contrast to the gay light colors of the angels' robes. The broad expanse of gold background, against which the devils stand out sharply in silhouette, is itself a daring feat. The subject matter of the icon suggests that it may have been made, not at, but for Mount Sinai; the icons that we can be fairly certain were executed there all are rougher in style. Thus it seems likely that this icon was made as a gift for the Sinai monastery, and we must again assume that Constantinople was the most likely place of origin.

24 In the twelfth century there was another change in style, this time to more solid, more monumental forms; eloquent evidence of this is an icon of Saint Euthymius in prayer. The monk stands his ground immovably and the figure is delineated in simple, even harsh outlines. Nothing distracts our eyes from the powerful head, all of whose details — the contracted brows, the long hooked nose, the tight lips — are keenly noted and full of character, but at the same time are abstractly impersonal. The saint's gaze is directed at a small bust of the Virgin, which resembles an icon and was in all likelihood conceived as such.

The further course of stylistic development in the twelfth century can be demonstrated very well by a type of icons which, at least until now, has not been found elsewhere than at Sinai. These are the beams of an iconostasis that were — and in part still are — placed like a frieze above the architrave; as a rule, they show beneath an arcade the representations of the twelve great feasts. In some instances the cycle of feasts is interrupted in the middle by a Deësis,[24] thereby repeating the theme of the large principal icons of the iconostasis; or it may be expanded by adding some scenes from the life of the Virgin at the beginning of the beam.[25] There are also beams showing scenes from the life of a saint, such as Saint Eustratius, one of the five martyrs of Sebaste;[26] a separate chapel is dedicated to this saint in the Sinai monastery and this work must certainly have been commissioned for that chapel. The earliest surviving beam depicts the twelve feasts
25, 26, 27 along with the Raising of Lazarus. It is in a style that tends toward monumentality, much like that of the icon of Saint Euthymius. Also typical are the almost rectangular contours which flatten the bodies but at the same time serve to integrate the individual figures firmly into the total compositional structure. Movement is confined within fixed limits and does not seem to arise out of any inner necessity; instead, it seems to be imposed from without. This is particularly noticeable in the head of Christ, which cranes far forward, and in the head of Peter, which inclines to one side: both movements are there for no other purpose than to conform to the curve of the framing arch above them. The color scale is strikingly light, almost pastel-like, and this is peculiar to this beam, distinguishing it from all the others.

The change of style in the latter half of the twelfth century can be seen in another beam on which it is apparent that more than one artist worked. To the first of those artists can be attributed
33 the Anastasis, or Descent into Limbo, which, in marked contrast to the measured calm of the Raising of Lazarus, is keyed to a high dramatic pitch. Christ strides ahead stormily to seize Adam by the wrist, while Adam leans forward to meet the Saviour with equal energy. The faces reveal a similar intensification of expression: Christ sharply scrutinizes Adam and Eve, whose eyes meet His in supplication. The change in the use of color is also typical: instead of luminous light colors, these are more saturated colors which radiate an inner glow and thereby add to the drama of the scene.

This emphasis on emotion began in the late Comnenian period, and it was accompanied by another new element: the observation of human relationships, which had previously been excluded from Byzantine art as alien to its essentially hieratic character. The earliest example that can be dated of this change of style, which was of such moment for the future development of Byzantine art, comes from 1164, or shortly after; it is the frescoes in Nerezi, in which the depiction of the Bewailing over the Dead Christ[27] has proved to be a key point in the study of this trend toward a more emotional expression. From that time on, the abundant material of fresco paintings, which are relatively easier to date, serves more and more to help us in dating icons, which, by their very nature, lack historical points of reference. Thus, fresco painting serves a similar function in our investigations of this period to that of miniature painting in the preceding phases of Middle Byzantine art.

The artist who painted the Descent into Limbo also began the Ascension, and completed the *32* left-side group of apostles headed by Saint Paul. Although the Saint Paul with his hand shading his eyes is traditional in type, the figure has been rendered dramatic, above all by the pleated mass of draperies whose agitated folds emphasize the exaggerated motion of the figure. Here the late Comnenian style takes a turn which has certain features in common with the Mannerist style of the sixteenth century.

The Virgin and the group of apostles on the right are attributed to a second artist, for the figures are conceived on a somewhat smaller scale and are much more slender. This is especially evident in the strikingly small heads, a detail which makes the parallel with sixteenth-century Mannerism even more obvious. The agitated drapery no longer follows the organic structure of the bodies, underlining their physical reality — as was still very much the case with Saint Paul — but instead it begins to have a life of its own. This is very noticeable in the swirl of drapery over the shoulder of the apostle seen from the rear. In a similar way the emotions expressed in the faces are exaggerated: the almost caricature-like sharpness of the profile of the apostle seen from behind, the disheveled hair of Saint Andrew, and the disproportionately high forehead of the apostle behind Peter (presumably Saint John) are characteristic. The ultimate phase, which carries all these elements to even more excess, is known to us from the frescoes in Kurbinovo in Macedonia, dated 1191,[28] and from those in the church of Laghoudera on Cyprus, from 1192.[29] Thus our beam can be dated about the seventh or eighth decade of the twelfth century.

However, the activity of this second artist was no more than an interlude. A third artist did the ascending Christ and the angels who bear aloft the circular mandorla, executed in the rotating technique used for nimbi; his style was more painterly than linear. This third painter also did the final scenes of the cycle of feasts: the Pentecost, and the Dormition of the Virgin. Out- *35* wardly the general impression is of greater calm. The turbulent treatment of the draperies is abandoned in favor of a much more simplified approach. However, the emotional element is not only retained, but has, in fact, been intensified through the coloristic means of a freer brush technique. One need only compare the Peter at the head of the bed in the Dormition with the same saint in the earlier Raising of Lazarus: the burning look with piercing eyes in the former is quite different from the fully formed but almost impassive expression in the latter, earlier, work. Instead of the traditional emphasis on strong local colors, the painter of the Dormition preferred subdued colors in sensitive nuances and tones such as olive-green which, by means of the symbolic values associated with colors, help bring out the funereal significance of the scene.

With this third, and latest, style of this beam (which today still forms part of an iconostasis although it is much later in date) we have perhaps passed beyond the time limit proposed. The origin of the artists who painted this cycle of feasts cannot even be guessed at in the present inadequate state of our knowledge of icon painting from that period. On the one hand, there can hardly be any doubt that each one of the stylistic phases of Middle Byzantine art that we have discussed had its origin in Constantinople. On the other hand, the style of the capital, beginning with the eleventh century, radiated into the provinces to such a degree that local differences either became assimilated or were suppressed. Today, historians of Byzantine art generally tend to ascribe to Constantinople all works of the highest quality and to hold the provincial centers responsible for anything of lesser quality. There are good grounds for assuming that Constantinople attracted the most talented artists, who set new standards for a high artistic level. However, in all times and places, the great metropolitan cities have also produced art of a lower artistic level, and for this reason we dare not go so far as to propose any more precise place of origin in the case of the beam from Sinai.

30   The stylistic phase of the second artist of this beam is found in another icon at Sinai, of such high quality that we cannot hesitate to attribute it to Constantinople. This is an Annunciation, whose almost monochromatic technique, imitating grisaille, is most unusual. Likewise uncommon is its iconography; in the foreground runs a river which we might take to be the symbolic form of one of the epithets of the Virgin, that of the "grace-giving stream." The approaching angel stops and turns round, creating with his double movement a "figura serpentinata." His searching look is directed at Mary and he seems to be struck by the thought that his sudden apparition may have alarmed her. Mary herself is not depicted as the stately matron of the traditional Annunciation in Byzantine art but rather as a frail maiden who meets the angel's glance with inner agitation and mild apprehension. The more subtle psychological observation, together with the elegant and sensitive drawing of the figures, renders this icon one of the most meaningful examples of late Comnenian art. Both of the fresco cycles mentioned above in connection with this particular stylistic phase (those of Kurbinovo and of Laghoudera) include an Annunciation which, in each case, is remarkably similar to that of our icon, but does not at all match it in quality. What is more, the figures on the icon (especially the angel) show a much more marked feeling for the organic form of the human body than do those of the frescoes, which tend more toward ornamentalized forms. All this suggests that the icon must have been painted in the capital. This gives us a clearer insight into the dependency of both Macedonian and Cypriot art upon the art of the capital, as well as the possibility of determining more sharply the peculiarities in the style of these peripheral centers.

The late Comnenian style exerted a profound influence not only on the Balkans and the countries east of Constantinople but also on the Latin West. It was correctly recognized long ago that the "maniera greca" of Guido da Siena and other Italian painters of the thirteenth century was derived from Byzantine models. However, all too rarely have Byzantine works been placed for comparison side by side with their contemporary Italian imitations. For this reason, our survey can best be concluded with two icons of the Virgin that represent types which, to a greater or lesser extent, served to inspire the entire art of Christendom of the time — the Orthodox as well as the Latin.

31   One of these shows the Virgin in prayer. This type of praying Virgin is designated as Hagiosoritissa[30] when only the single figure is depicted; but in this case we are probably dealing with one icon belonging to a group of three — the Virgin, together with Christ and John the Baptist — which constituted a Deësis originally decorating an iconostasis. The heavily shadowed eyes and slightly frowning eyebrows create an impression of gentle melancholy like that in the well-known icon, the Virgin of Vladimir, now in Moscow. Here the expression is truly spiritual, a premonition perhaps of the suffering the future holds in store for Son and Mother alike. This degree of inner intensity is peculiar to the best Byzantine icons but was rarely attained by imitations in Italy or elsewhere, however great their formal achievement may have been at times.

36   Our second example is another icon of the Virgin, this time of the so-called Odegitria type, whose archetype was a full-length standing figure,[31] but here we have a half-length figure; what is more, this one is executed in the subtle technique of mosaic wax ground which in the Middle Byzantine period came to be frequently used for the most precious portable icons. The cubes of mosaic are so minute (especially in the face and hands) that they can hardly be made out by the naked eye. This means that the feeling for the material of mosaic was to some degree sacrificed in the imitation of brush technique. On the other hand, the special virtues of the mosaic medium are amply exploited in the gold highlights of the drapery folds, and in the background pattern which imitates cloisonné enamels. In contrast to older iconographic tradition, the Virgin here inclines

her head slightly toward the Child; this gives the image a somewhat human feeling, but her gaze does not meet that of the Child. This brings out clearly the basic postulate of orthodoxy, which limits icon painting to the sphere of the hieratic and transcendental. After a certain period, it was these limitations which artists of the Latin West no longer respected. The weightless pose of the Child, seated so unsteadily on the Virgin's arm that He almost seems to be about to slide off, belongs within the same hieratic convention. Such abstractions are the fundamental presuppositions in icon painting, which aims at a stronger, more religious power of conviction.

We are all too conscious of having given only the most sketchy outline of icon painting from the sixth to the twelfth century. For this we have depended entirely on material preserved in the Monastery of Saint Catherine on Mount Sinai, where the largest body of icons from those centuries has survived.[32] The very few icons known from that period which have been found elsewhere can for the most part be traced back to this monastery. Be that as it may, it would be wrong to assume that the collection on Mount Sinai can give us a complete cross-section of the history of icon painting in the centuries here discussed. Even if it could be proved that, as we have proposed, the two finest icons of the sixth and seventh centuries actually came from Constantinople, certain questions would still remain unanswered. We do not yet know what the icons from Constantinople were really like at the end of the seventh and the beginning of the eighth century; nor do we know whether icons were in fact produced in the capital and the Byzantine empire proper in the interval between the two phases of the Iconoclast ban on images, or even what the style of the first icons may have been after the defeat of the Iconoclasts. Furthermore, even if our hypothesis that there was a separate School of Jerusalem should be proved correct, it would not alter the fact that Jerusalem was only one of a number of centers where icons were made and that there must have been other centers of equal importance which cannot as yet be traced.

If it is a step forward in our knowledge to have identified a few icons as belonging to the tenth century, it must be admitted that they fail to live up to our expectations with respect to that flourishing century. Only in the eleventh century does the Sinai material become sufficiently abundant to permit one to hope that some day it may be possible to reconstruct a coherent history of the development of icon painting of this period. Only then will we be able to lay down the bases for a clearer formulation of just how the style of Constantinople — which is more or less synonymous with that of Byzantium as a whole — made its influence felt within the neighboring countries, especially in those of the Balkans which lie so close to this great center of the past.

Notes, Part I

1 Much has been written about the Iconoclast controversy. The references here have been chosen from
writings by art historians concerned with the icons
that have survived from that time: A. GRABAR,
Martyrium, Recherches sur le culte des reliques et
l'art chrétien antique, II, Paris, 1946, pp. 343 ff.;
idem, L'Iconoclasme byzantin, Dossier archéologique,
Paris, 1957; E. KITZINGER, The Cult of Images in the
Age before Iconoclasm, Dumbarton Oaks Papers,
VIII, 1954, pp. 85 ff.

2 Д. Айналоь, Синайскія Икона Восковой живопи-
си, in: Византиский Временник, IX, 1902, pp. 343 ff.,
Plates I-V

3 G. and M. SOTIRIOU, Icônes du Mont Sinai, I (Plates),
1956, II (Text), 1958

4 O. RUBENSOHN, Aus griechisch-römischen Häusern
des Fayum, Jahrb. d. Arch. Inst., XX, 1905, pp. 16
ff., pls. 1-3

5 R. PAGENSTECHER, Klapptafelbild, Votivtriptychon
und Flügelaltar, Arch. Anz., XXXIV, 1919, pp. 9 ff.,
figs. 1-4

6 Since writing this, a third masterpiece of the early
period has been revealed under later overpainting, an
icon of a bust of Christ, published by M. CHATZIDAKIS
in Art Bulletin, 1967

7 H. ZALOSCER, Porträts aus dem Wüstensand, die
Mumienbildnisse aus der Oase Fayum, Vienna, 1961,
fig. 2

8 E. KITZINGER, op. cit., p. 90

9 K. A. NEUGEBAUER, Die Familie des Septimius Severus, Die Antike, XII, pp. 155 ff., pls. 10-11

10 That disc-shaped icons were still common in the
ninth and tenth centuries is shown by certain miniatures in the Vatican Menologion and by a few mar-
ginal psalters. Cf. A. GRABAR, L'Iconoclasme byzantin, pp. 219 ff., figs. 139 ff.

11 R. DELBRUECK, Die Consulardiptychen und verwandte
Denkmäler, Berlin-Leipzig, 1929, nos. 19-21 (Anthe-
mius and Anastasius)

12 The same motif is found on a sixth-century ivory
plaque, presumably from Syria, the so-called Murano

Diptych in the Museum of Antiquities in Ravenna.
W. F. VOLBACH, Elfenbeinarbeiten der Spätantike
und des frühen Mittelalters, Mainz, 1952, p. 64,
no. 125, pl. 39

13 For an attempt to relate a pre-Iconoclastic group of
icons with Jerusalem as the most probable place of
origin, cf. K. WEITZMANN, The Jephthah Panel in the
Bema of the Church of St. Catherine's on Mount Sinai,
Dumbarton Oaks Papers, XVIII, 1964, pp. 341 ff

14 For the archaic inscription Η ΑΓΙΑ ΜΑΡΙΑ and a
criticism of the thesis that it was limited to Egyptian
art, see K. WEITZMANN, Eine vorikonoklastische Ikone
des Sinai mit der Darstellung des Chairete, Festschrift
Johannes Kollwitz; TORTULAC, Studien zu altchrist-
lichen und byzantinischen Monumenten, Röm.
Quartalschrift, 30. Supplementheft, 1966

15 From the extensive bibliography of recent years on
the subject of Christ on the Cross with closed eyes,
I shall cite only one study because it corrects the
late dating proposed by Grondijs. J. R. MARTIN, The
Dead Christ on the Cross in Byzantine Art, Late
Classical and Medieval Studies in Honor of A. M.
Friend, Jr., Princeton, 1955, pp. 189 ff.

16 J. WILPERT, Die römischen Mosaiken und Malereien
der kirchlichen Bauten vom IV.-VIII. Jahrhundert, II,
p. 687; IV, pl. 180. E. KITZINGER, Römische Malerei
vom Beginn des 7. bis zur Mitte des 8. Jahrhunderts,
Munich (dissertation), 1934, pp. 26 ff.

17 K. WEITZMANN, Geistige Grundlagen und Wesen der
Makedonischen Renaissance, Arbeitsgemeinschaft für
Forschung des Landes Nordrhein-Westfalen, Geistes-
wissenschaft series, no. 107, Cologne, 1963 (with
previous bibliography on this subject)

18 These appeared with all their luminosity only after
the icon was cleaned by Carroll Wales, the restorer
for the Alexandria-Michigan-Princeton expedition

19 A. GOLDSCHMIDT and K. WEITZMANN, Die byzantinischen Elfenbeinskulpturen des X.-XIII. Jahrhunderts,
II, Berlin, 1934, pp. 13 ff., 25 ff., and pls. I-IX.
In the present context we are concerned with the
ivories of the so-called "painterly group"

20 A. Pasini, Il tesoro di San Marco in Venezia, Venice, 1885, pls. II, IV, XXIII

21 G. and M. Sotiriou, op. cit., I, pls. 165-70

22 The most comprehensive cycles known belong precisely to the eleventh century: the Paris codex Bibl. Nat. gr. 74 (cf. H. Omont, Evangiles avec peintures byzantines du XIe siècle, Paris, n. d.) and the Florentine codex Laurenziana Plut. VI, 23 (cf. G. Millet, Iconographie de l'Evangile, Paris, 1916, passim)

23 J. R. Martin, The Illustration of the Heavenly Ladder of John Climacus, Princeton, 1954, is a study of the collected illustrated manuscripts of this work

24 G. and M. Sotiriou, op. cit., I, pls. 95-96, 113, 115

25 Ibid., I, pls. 99, 101, 125

26 Ibid., I, pls. 103-111; II, pp. 109 ff.

27 N. L. Okunev, La Découverte des anciennes fresques du monastère de Nerez, Slavia: Časopis pro Slovanskou Filologii, VI, 1927-28, pp. 603 ff.; G. Millet and A. Frolow, La Peinture du moyen-âge en Yougoslavie, Fasc. I, Paris, 1954, pls. 15-21; A. Grabar, Byzantine Painting, Geneva, 1953, p. 141 and fig. p. 143; O. Bihalji-Merin, Fresken und Ikonen: Mittelalterliche Kunst in Serbien und Makedonien, Munich, 1958, pl. 26

28 R. Ljubinković, Stara crkva sela Kurbinovo, Starinar, XV, 1940, pp. 101 ff.; G. Millet and A. Frolow, op. cit., pls. 84-85

29 Ἀ. Στυλιανοῦ, Αἱ τοιχογραφίαι τοῦ ναοῦ τῆς Παναγίας τοῦ Ἀράχου, Λαγουδερά, Κύπρος, Perpragmena, IXe Congrès international des études byzantines, Salonica, 1953, Athens, 1955, pp. 459 ff. and pls. 142-57; A. H. S. Megaw, Comnenian Frescoes in Cyprus, XIIe Congrès international des études byzantines, Ohrida, 1961, Résumé des communications, p. 69

30 S. Der Nersessian, Two Images of the Virgin in the Dumbarton Oaks Collection, Dumbarton Oaks Papers, XIV, 1960, pp. 77 ff.

31 One of the earliest examples of the full-length Odegitria is one of the title miniatures of the Syrian Rabula Codex from A.D. 586. C. Cecchelli, G. Furlani, and M. Salmi, The Rabbula Gospels, Olten, 1959, folio 1 verso

32 All photographs of the Sinai icons published in this essay were made by the Alexandria-Michigan-Princeton expedition to Mount Sinai, headed by Professor George Forsyth, of the University of Michigan, and the author, of Princeton University, during four campaigns between 1958 and 1965. The photographic supervision and execution were in the hands of Mr. Fred Anderegg of the University of Michigan

List of Icons, Part I

1 VIRGIN ENTHRONED BETWEEN SAINT THEODORE AND SAINT GEORGE. 6th century. Encaustic. 27×18⁷/₈″. Monastery of Saint Catherine, Sinai

2 VIRGIN. Detail, plate 1

3 ANGEL. Detail, plate 1

5 SAINT PETER. 7th century. Encaustic. 36¹/₂×21″. Monastery of Saint Catherine, Sinai

6 CRUCIFIXION. 8th century. 18¹/₄×10″. Monastery of Saint Catherine, Sinai

7 THE THIEF GESTAS. Detail, plate 6

8 ANGEL. Detail, plate 9

9 THE THREE HEBREWS IN THE FIERY FURNACE. c. 7th century. Encaustic. 13¹/₄×19¹/₂″. Monastery of Saint Catherine, Sinai

11 THE APOSTLE THADDEUS. 10th century. Wing of a triptych. Height of the whole wing, 11″ (this figure occupies a little more than half); width 3³/₄″. Monastery of Saint Catherine, Sinai

13 SAINTS ZOSIMUS AND NICHOLAS. 10th century. 8¹/₈×5¹/₂″. Monastery of Saint Catherine, Sinai

14 HEAD OF THE APOSTLE PHILIP. Detail, plate 15

15 THE APOSTLE PHILIP. 10th-11th centuries. 12⁷/₈×8″. Monastery of Saint Catherine, Sinai

16 SAINT NICHOLAS. 10th-11th centuries. 16⁷/₈×13″. Monastery of Saint Catherine, Sinai

17 VIRGIN AND TWO SCENES FROM THE LIFE OF SAINT NICHOLAS. c. 11th century. Fragment of a wing of a triptych. 8⁵/₈×4³/₄″. Monastery of Saint Catherine, Sinai

19 THE LADDER TO HEAVEN OF JOHN CLIMACUS. 11th-12th centuries. 16¹/₈×11¹/₂″. Monastery of Saint Catherine, Sinai

21 CRUCIFIXION. 11th-12th centuries. 11¹/₈×8¹/₂″. Monastery of Saint Catherine, Sinai

22 MASSACRE OF THE INNOCENTS. Detail, plate 23

23 NATIVITY AND INFANCY OF CHRIST. 11th century. 14¹/₄×8³/₈″. Monastery of Saint Catherine, Sinai

24 SAINT EUTHYMIUS. 12th century. 24³/₄×16¹/₈″. Monastery of Saint Catherine, Sinai

25 RAISING OF LAZARUS. 12th century. Scene from an iconostasis beam. Width of panel containing three scenes, 16¹/₈×44¹/₂″. Monastery of Saint Catherine, Sinai

26 CHRIST WITH APOSTLES. Detail, plate 25

27 LAZARUS. Detail, plate 25

28 THE APOSTLE JAMES. Detail, plate 29

29 TRANSFIGURATION. 12th century. On the same iconostasis beam as plates 25-27. Monastery of Saint Catherine, Sinai

30 ANNUNCIATION. End of 12th century. c. 22¹/₂×16¹/₂″. Monastery of Saint Catherine, Sinai

31 VIRGIN IN PRAYER. c. 1200. 29⁵/₈×20¹/₈″. Monastery of Saint Catherine, Sinai

32 ASCENSION OF CHRIST. End of 12th or beginning of 13th century. On the same iconostasis beam as plates 33 and 35. 15×10¹/₄″. Monastery of Saint Catherine, Sinai

33 DESCENT INTO LIMBO. End of 12th century. On the same iconostasis beam as plates 32 and 35. 15¹/₄×21¹/₂″ (panel includes two scenes). Monastery of Saint Catherine, Sinai.

35 DORMITION OF THE VIRGIN. End of 12th or beginning of 13th century. On the same iconostasis beam as plates 32 and 33. 15¹/₈×10¹/₈″. Monastery of Saint Catherine, Sinai

36 VIRGIN AND CHILD. c. 1200. Mosaic. 17¹/₂×13″. Monastery of Saint Catherine, Sinai

1

2

6

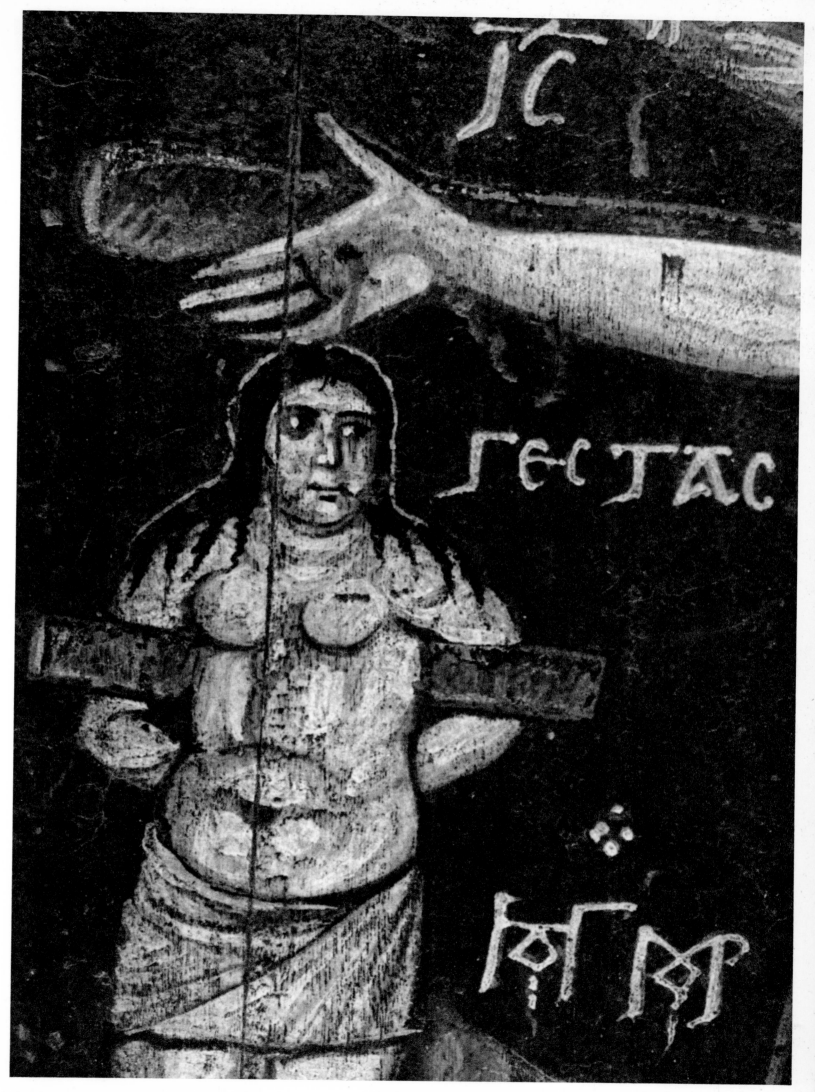

8

13

14

16

28

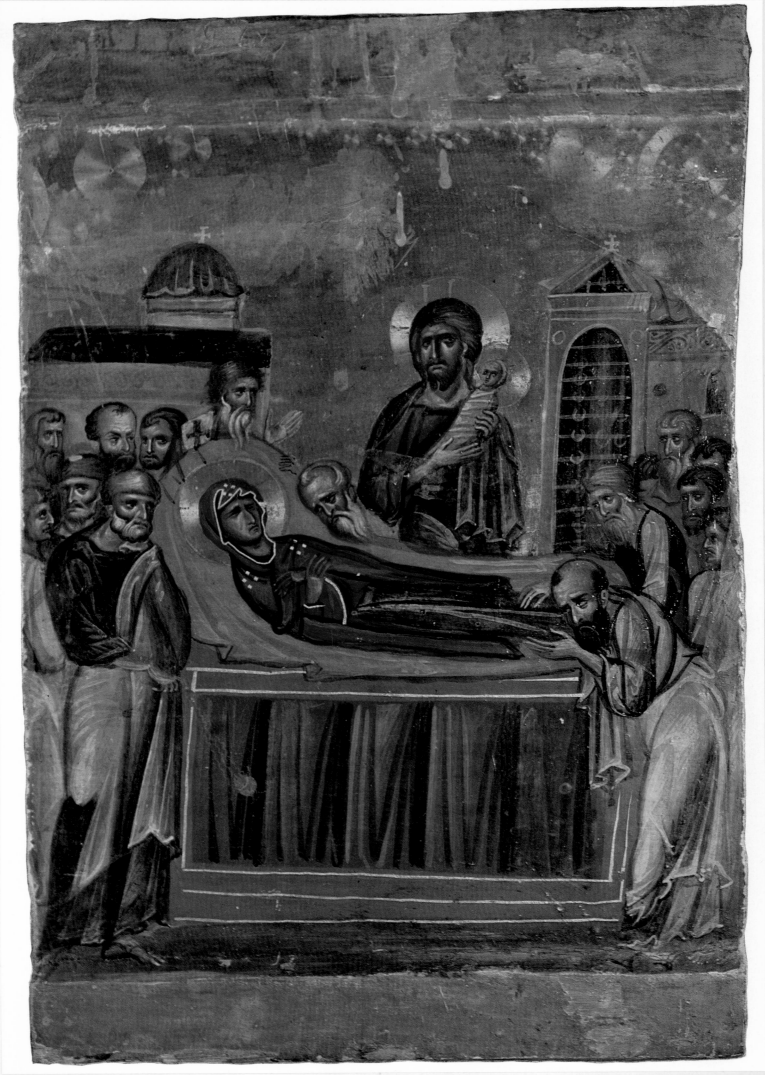

35

II. GREECE

Icon Painting from the Twelfth to the Sixteenth Century *by Manolis Chatzidakis*

Plates 37—96

Among the Byzantine icons found in Greece today, scarcely a single category can be defined which originated, to any degree of certainty, within the boundaries of the political and geographical entity we now call Greece. But in the Byzantine period — the time before Constantinople fell to the Turks — there was at least one important center of artistic production which is part of Greece today: Salonica. The contribution of Salonica, especially in the time of the Palaeologues, is becoming increasingly clear. Many of the icons reproduced in these pages come from the churches of that great city and can consequently be considered to have been produced there; this claim is borne out in the majority of cases by comparison with other works whose origin was certainly Salonica. Mount Athos cannot be considered an artistic center with a definite character of its own; the icons found there in recent years belong to many diverse artistic currents. There were other centers in Greece, such as Arta, Jannina, and Mistra, but their artistic independence remains to be established. It seems likely that the art of these minor capitals of late and ephemeral principalities merely reflected what was being done in more important places. We can speak fairly surely of a School of Cyprus; but when it comes to Crete, whose mural painting of the fourteenth and fifteenth centuries is now better known, we can only hypothesize about the field of icon painting.

Icons, being a portable form of art, easily make their way from one locality to another. Thus we can say with some assurance that some of the works dealt with here must have come initially from Constantinople. Not only was Constantinople the chief city of Byzantium, but we also see it as the central source from which a great art spread to the Imperial territories and through the entire sphere of Byzantine influence. It is because of this that we have not hesitated to discuss certain icons which were not found in Greece but belong to the sphere of Byzantine art.

For these reasons, our aim here can only be to consider all icons purely and simply as works of Byzantine art, not concerning ourselves with whether they belong to some regional school. All these remarks apply, however, only to icons made before 1453, when Constantinople was conquered by the Turks. The icons reproduced here from the sixteenth and seventeenth centuries can be traced with absolute certainty to Crete, or to Cretan artists working abroad. After the collapse of the Imperial center, the great tradition was carried on in the outlying regions.

The icons presented here do not typify all the aspects to be found in Greek works. Instead we have attempted to select pieces that represent various trends; we have also included a certain number that are less well known but better preserved or which, at least, have been recently restored. In any event, we hope there have been no serious omissions.

Icons dating from the twelfth century are rare in Greece. It might have been expected that there would be more in the great monastic centers, as in the case of the Monastery of Saint Catherine in Sinai. In recent years the cataloguing and restoration carried out by the Greek Archaeological Service have brought to light a number of icons in the monasteries on Mount Athos; most of them survived because they had been discarded in inaccessible places and, in any case, were no longer in use. It would be interesting to compare these icons with those found in the Sinai monastery, but their number is as yet insufficient to make possible a broad, general study. We shall not hesitate to consider them, however, where appropriate.

42   Among the oldest icons that are relatively well preserved is the small icon of Saint Panteleimon in the Monastery of Lavra. The face of the handsome young intercessor clearly recalls that of the famous icon, the Virgin of Vladimir. The large almond-shaped eyes, arched eyebrows, small mouth, fine nose, and lastly the tender yet dignified expression with its slightly sideways glance — all classify this icon within the same group as the Vladimir Virgin. The formal conception, the emphasis on line, and the part played by color in the delicate modeling achieved by greenish shadows and rosy flesh are common to both works.

41   Another icon, monumental in its dimensions, is that of Saint Peter in the Protaton on Mount Athos. The apostle's pose recalls that usually given to large figures of the prophets holding open scrolls. This is one of the most important icons of the late Comnenian period, and it shows the influence of monumental mural art upon icon painting at that time. The features, however, are drawn with a calligraphic attention to clear linear values which is not without a certain academicism.

    The same feeling for monumentality is found in the scenes from a Dodecaorton, a cycle of icons
37 for the twelve great feast days; an example is this small icon with the Raising of Lazarus. The rather thickset but well-modeled figures form a composition of monumental character belying the small dimensions of the icon. The figure of Christ near the center is dominant not only through its more imposing stature and larger head, but also by its isolation and its expressive intensity. The setting and landscape elements are reduced to a minimum, yet the rather somber coloring of the figures — ranging through shades of blue combined with purplish red and ocher — stands out markedly against the vermilion background. The same, rather rare type of background occurs in a small icon of the Transfiguration now in the Russian Museum, Leningrad, and the icon belongs to the same cycle of church feasts as our Raising of Lazarus. These two works, however, have more in common than their red backgrounds and similar dimensions: they share stylistic peculiarities and even something individualistic in manner which permit us to attribute them to the same artist. The Leningrad work has been assigned to the twelfth century by Wulff, Lazarev, and Bank, and indeed the predominating monumentality of both icons is typical of the twelfth century. There is further evidence in the treatment of the faces: the features are drawn clearly and the brownish flesh tones are built up rather freely through graduated shades of color, and white streaks on the salient features contrast with red brush strokes on the cheeks and foreheads. The same kind of modeling is found in the Nerezi fresco of 1164, and in the Christ of manuscript 2645 (in the National Library, Athens) which was painted before 1206. Yet a certain stiffness in the draperies as well as the peculiar proportions of the figures suggest that both our icons might be better dated around the beginning of the thirteenth century.

    The recognition that two such icons as the Raising of Lazarus and the Transfiguration, now far apart, must belong to the same series of icons forming a Dodecaorton implies that, during the twelfth and thirteenth centuries, such series celebrating the twelve feast days of the Church must have been grouped together in a place above the iconostasis as a unified cycle of related pictures.

    It seems, however, that the more common way of representing the feasts was to paint the separate scenes on an architrave generally carved out of a single beam of wood. One such architrave,
43 found in the Monastery of Vatopedi, depicts the Christ Pantocrator enthroned in the center of a Great Deësis. The side sections of the architrave bear the scenes from the Gospels appropriate to the cycle of feasts. This manner of arranging the iconostasis used to be known only in Sinai, from the twelfth century on, but it is now established that the gradual transformation of the

iconostasis through the use of such painted wooden architraves must have taken place in a great cultural center; this was surely Constantinople, and from there it spread to Athos and Sinai. The painting on the Vatopedi architrave, having the reduced dimensions of a miniature, is related to manuscript illumination in style. This applies to almost all works of the sort. A more delicate manner of painting and greater refinement of expression show that icon painting retained certain qualities peculiar to itself despite the predominant influence of monumental mural art. Actually, the head of Christ, despite its majesty, is modeled with rich nuances showing a range of gradations from the delicate green shadows to the bright rose highlights of the skin. The effect of relief is not achieved through excessive emphasis on contrasts and line, and this brings out the very human beauty of the Redeemer's face by refined painterly means.

There were still other approaches to artistic expression during the thirteenth century. A double-faced icon, now in the Byzantine Museum at Athens, has interesting features that reveal the vicissitudes an icon may undergo through the impact of a country's diverse historical events. At the same time, it affords us a glimpse of one significant moment in the evolution of the iconic style. One side of the icon shows a Virgin and Child from the sixteenth century. The other side, of particular interest here, has a Crucifixion showing a peculiar mixture of styles wholly lacking in unity. Only since its recent restoration has it been possible to explain that there are contributions from three distinct periods: from the earliest, the ninth century, to the latest, the thirteenth. The head of Christ and the figures of the Virgin and Saint John belong to the third period. They are superior in quality to what survives from the earliest painting which is still markedly linear and of crude workmanship. They are freely modeled in tones of sienna and brighter highlights, and surrounded by slightly green shadows. In these faces we can recognize the attempt to render emotion, even pathos, and yet exaggeration is always avoided. The barely suggested grimace of grief, the narrow form of the shadow around Christ's eyes, the continuous curve of John's eyebrows which parallels the hair-line across his forehead, the deep furrow down his cheek — all of these simple devices serve the representation of the fundamental psychic stresses, namely, suffering and grief. And yet, in spite of the conciseness of these expressive means, which do not lack a certain rhythm of their own, we feel a remarkable power of observation on the artist's part. These qualities still have much in common with the outburst of pathos in the Nerezi fresco of 1164 but are more restrained and more profound, as also befits the nature of icons. *44, 45, 46*

A similar conception is found in another double-faced icon, this one from Cyprus, also with a Virgin and Child on one side and a Crucifixion on the other. The ornamentation in relief for the haloes and backgrounds is evidence that it comes from a local workshop. A certain elegance in the postures, the delicacy of tension, and the transparency of the subtly varied colors suggest an environment on a cultivated level that was subject to Western influences; likewise indicative are such iconographic details as the transparent loincloth of Christ. These features suggest Cyprus, which was occupied by the French as early as 1192. *47*

Although one of these icons came from Epirus and was later found (after who knows what vicissitudes) in a small monastery near Arta, and the other came from Cyprus, they are both contemporary works, and it is not too much to call attention to a certain obvious relationship between them. They provide additional and especially convincing evidence of the strength of the new artistic currents emanating from the great centers of culture, and of the rapid spread of such trends to every corner of the Byzantine territories, including the other lands under Byzantine influence. As for their dating, it is difficult to ascertain if they should be ascribed to the period when Constantinople was occupied by the French in 1204, or to the years following its liberation in 1261. In any case, it seems more likely that such innovations came from the great capital rather than from the small provincial centers that were merely capitals of minor principalities — as, for instance, Arta in the despotate of Epirus.

These two icons present us with a phenomenon that was destined — either through its presence or its absence — to become a key factor in the formation and development of style in Byzantine painting, and most of all in the icon. This factor is the direct contact between Byzantium and the West; it came about through the great movements which changed the course of history, notably the Crusades. Constantinople was occupied only temporarily, between 1204 and 1261, but such provinces as Crete, Cyprus, and the Peloponnesus were definitely won for the West. The icon *44, 45, 46* in the Byzantine Museum can stand for the type of Byzantine art which provided a Giunta Pisano *47* or a Coppo di Marcovaldo with models for their Crucifixions. On the other hand, the Cyprus icon, with its pronounced occidental traits, is a typical example of the Western influences on Byzantine art, especially in Western-occupied provinces such as Crete; in frescoes in small country chapels of Crete we often find Western influences — haloes with ornamentation in relief and European fashions in costume and armor.

49 To this region and period belongs another double-faced icon, also in the Byzantine Museum, with scenes from the life and martyrdom of Saint George. This icon comes from Castoria and has a rather uncommon feature: the figure of the saint is carved like a relief in the wood of the icon, and so are his halo and shield. His military costume and the design of the shield with its four fields are Western in character, but the inscription, rather well drawn in pseudo-cufic letters around the border of the shield, seems to indicate as place of origin some region close to the Moslem East. The figure itself, lacking elegance and stiffly posed, is quite unlike the Byzantine sculpture of the time. Instinctively one thinks of Romanesque art, in which sculptures and, especially, icons in high relief are common. Stone icons carved in relief were not unknown in Byzantine art of earlier periods, and there are even examples in precious materials, such as the two famous icons of the Archangel Michael in gold and enamel in the Cathedral Treasury of Saint Mark in Venice, which were made during the tenth or eleventh century. But Byzantine wooden specimens, carved in relief and painted, are rare. One enormous icon, over nine feet high, with Saint George depicted frontally and at full length, is in Omorphi Ekklisia near Castoria; another, presumably of Saint Clement, is in Ohrid; a few more pieces of lesser importance are practically all that are known. Our task of determining their place of origin is not made easier by the fact that these works come from, or are found at present, in regions where there is scarcely any trace of Western influence.

The painted images on this Byzantine Museum icon, which complement the figure of Saint George, may assist us in our task. There are six scenes on either side of the saint, twelve in all, plus two angels above him and a small figure of the female donor prostrate behind his feet. They are painted in a free, almost impressionistic manner, with green shadows, rosy cheeks, and tiny gleaming white highlights; they resemble thirteenth-century miniatures (compare Ms. Iviron 5, Berlin Qu 66). But the types of figures and a certain mannerism in their postures suggest rather a comparison with the art of the Latin Kingdom of Jerusalem. The two saints on the reverse side of this icon, although poorly preserved, remind us of certain figures of the Virgin from thirteenth-century Cyprus with their large eyes and broad modeling with subtle nuances. We would willingly assign this icon either to Jerusalem or to Cyprus, the connections between these centers being not yet sufficiently clear. In any case, this solid figure of Saint George with its simplified surfaces belongs to the trend toward monumentality already noted, a trend which — in addition to foreign influences — continued throughout thirteenth-century icon painting, both in single figures and scenes.

39 An icon from Patmos contains a half-length figure of Saint James. An air of serene majesty emanates from this beautiful, broadly modeled, solid figure with its simple rhythmic draperies and lively coloring, suggesting that its prototype may have been a large statuesque figure like the apostles in the frescoes at Sopoćani. The icon may belong to the same period as the frescoes, around 1265, and to the same spiritual climate full of classical reminiscences. It offers important support for our argument that the monumental style of the thirteenth century was not foreign to the panel painting of the time.

There can be no doubt that, from the point of view of style, icon painting was closely bound with monumental painting. There is, however, one type of portable icon which directly reflects the influence of the monumental style even in material and technique. These are mosaic icons, many of which still survive in Greece at Mount Athos, Patmos, the Monastery of Tatrana, and in the Byzantine Museum of Athens. The oldest mosaic icons from the eleventh and twelfth centuries — such as those in the Patriarchate of Constantinople, or the icon of the Virgin in the Monastery of Chilandar — have the normal dimensions of icons. The size of the mosaic cubes and the technique that was used hardly differ from those of contemporary wall mosaics. These mosaic icons were intended for marble iconostases (to which their material was better suited than painted wood) and for proskynitaria. As was usual in images intended for liturgical use, they generally present a half-length figure. Later, in the thirteenth century, mosaic technique began to take on certain traits more closely related to icon painting, and it became, about 1300, a vehicle for virtuoso display: the icons were reduced to the smallest possible size, and the mosaic stones were as tiny as grains of sand. In addition, the icon often became a luxurious object in itself, encased in a cover of precious metal sometimes decorated with cloisonné insets. These general observations are enough to show us that these icons originated in the aristocratic circles of the capital, if not in the Imperial Palace itself.

At the beginning of the fourteenth century, mosaic icons were further distinguished by the fact that they often included entire scenes, among these the Twelve Feasts of the Church, the Annunciation, the Transfiguration, the Crucifixion, the Forty Martyrs, or saints on foot or on horseback. In the Palaeologue period, life-size figures in half-length continued to be produced for liturgical use, and remained very similar to mosaic wall decorations. We show here the icon of Saint Nicholas 57 in the Monastery of Stavronikita on Mount Athos; it is not a virtuoso work like the miniature mosaic icons, but is composed of glass cubes of the usual size — although very tiny tesserae were used at that time even in monumental wall mosaics. In technique, style, and quality this work can be compared with certain figures in the mosaics, of 1315, in the Church of the Holy Apostles at Salonica. The Prophet Jonah is especially similar to Saint Nicholas: they have the same shape of brow, and of eyes, nose, and mouth; the same broad planes are highlighted by lines of warmer tones that complement each other and contrast in a free, almost impressionistic manner with the greenish shadows. This technique, so supremely apt for mosaic, contributes a certain animation to the modeling of the venerable figure of Saint Nicholas, in his traditional hieratic pose; the broad white homophorion with its large black crosses and the blue vestment lend a coolness of tone to the entire icon. On the basis of these facts, it is not too much to conclude that the work was produced in Salonica at the beginning of the fourteenth century.

Another icon of this sort, now in the Byzantine Museum, comes from Triglia in Bithynia. The 51 Virgin holding the Child on one arm belongs to the type known as Glykophilousa or Eleousa ("Virgin of the Sweet Embrace" or "Virgin of Compassion") and the icon bears the inscription in mosaic: Μήτηρ Θεοῦ ἡ Ἐπίσκεψις. From this evidence it is probable that this icon is a copy of another icon similarly titled. The fact that it is not the conventional bust but a half-length figure suggests that the Virgin must have appeared full length in the original. Tenderness and affection are seen in the picture despite a certain rigidity resulting from specifically formal elements: the firm rhythmic treatment of the draperies and the closed symmetrical composition using broad curves. These characteristics were probably derived from the prototype, which must have been of top quality, and they were not very successfully copied here. The drawing of the faces is somewhat crude and the feet of the Child clumsy, betraying a want of sensitivity. Yet this deficiency is effectively masked by the brilliant coloring with gold highlights on the dark draperies, and by the richness of the mosaic material itself. The author of this early fourteenth-century mosaic icon must have been, all things considered, a craftsman rather than an artist.

48   To a quite different type of mosaic icon belongs the miniature icon exhibited for the first time in Athens, 1964, in the exhibition of Byzantine art; it came from the small, now-ruined monastery of Tatarna in central Greece. In this half-length figure of the crucified Christ, the beautiful head with abundant hair and noble features with closed eyes are delineated by narrow streaks. His body is relatively broad, with strong shoulders, while His arms, insofar as they are visible, hang slack and wasted. It was typical of Palaeologue art that when it aimed to arouse compassion, it exploited the opposition of masses in order to stress the contrasts inherent in them: the massive body against the emaciated arms, the spirituality of the long, narrow face against the wild growth of hair, the impression of robust strength against the feeling of isolation in death. We often find these same motifs in other Crucifixions of the time, such as the example at Ohrid which is usually dated as the end of the thirteenth century. There are many similarities between this icon and the mosaic icon in the Church of Santa Croce in Gerusalemme in Rome, in which Christ is likewise portrayed half-length with head sharply inclined, but with crossed arms. In all probability, the two works had a common prototype.

72   Finally, in a mosaic icon of Saint Demetrius in Sassoferrato, the tall, slender figure has that unstable pose which we find in the seemingly weightless figures typical of painting after the middle of the fourteenth century, the formal symbol of an aristocratic, even effete, youth. The face, modeled with extremely fine cubes of mosaic, is expressionless, almost indifferent, but it nevertheless belongs to a type familiar to us from the patron saints of Salonica. The frail and elegant figure and the background are overladen with geometrical decorative elements, such as the star-shaped, interlocking squares containing the name of the saint, the cross-grid pattern of the halo which reappears in larger form on the pavement tiles, and the fine checkerboard of the leg guards. A diagonal is formed by the edge of the mantle, the left-hand border of the shield, and the sword belt that, with the help of the lance, cuts the picture into two triangles of almost equal shape. The impression of a mixture of heterogeneous elements is reinforced by the lion on the shield that is at once heraldic and realistic in treatment — and, in both respects, decidedly Western. It is not difficult, therefore, to date this delicately wrought but eclectic work toward the end of the fourteenth century, since it reveals a fully formed and self-confident style that is free to pick and choose its means.

    One of the fundamental traits of icons, insofar as religious personages are represented, is that the likeness is based by theoretical principle on a true or accepted resemblance to the prototype. In a famous phrase, Saint Basil used the word "prototype" to designate the sacred personage, but it can also be used in its modern meaning. Since divine grace of the icon is transmitted through its resemblance to the personage depicted, that grace is perpetuated in icons which resemble their prototype — that is, the original icon — to the extent that they copy it faithfully. One might expect, then, that once the likeness of a saint had been established — which happened especially after the Iconoclast controversy — it would be repeated endlessly without change. But the fact is that Byzantine art was a living art closely linked to historical circumstances and, above all, to the spiritual currents of its time. Thus the sensibility of its artists was able to find endless forms of expression for the same subjects, not only from one period to another but also within a single period.

    In both theory and practice the Byzantine portrait aimed only at reproducing the general characteristics of the personage depicted. We know this from texts that, although unofficial, nevertheless reflect Byzantine thought on this matter. Among these are the remarkable writings of Elpios, a Roman who lived in the ninth and tenth centuries. His text describes the most important sacred personages, for the most part, in detail; the others are described more succinctly. There are also descriptions of saints found in their biographies and in the Synaxaria, or, finally, in the later editions of the Herminia, the book from which Byzantine painters took the accepted formulas for their depictions. From the practical point of view, it was necessary for the worshiper to be able to recognize the saint depicted at sight, through certain essential characteristics, without having to read the inscription. This was actually the case with the better-known saints. Once these requirements had been fulfilled, the rest was left up to the painter in accordance with the ruling of the Seventh Council that only the art belongs to the painter, but the exact disposition (διάταξις) is to be decided by the Holy Fathers. However, the painter worked with technical procedures and within aesthetic traditions which went back to the Hellenistic-Roman period and Late Antiquity. Traces of these origins of Christian portraiture can be discerned throughout the entire development of Byzantine painting. The tendency of Byzantine painters to allow the real to become permeated by the unreal culminated in the transfiguration of the human figure into a Christian image, and in a transformation of the language of art. But whatever the painter might do, the fundamental basis remained the same, and the painter merely approached it or departed from it. Icons depicting saints afforded the artist the possibility of maintaining the abstraction, or of infusing the abstract image with an individual content and thus turning the icon into a true portrait. A series of icons from the fourteenth century is instructive in showing the variety of ways in which the painters of that time carried out their task, and how they adapted natural forms to represent the unreal world of their ideals.

As an example, an icon from the Monastery of Vatopedi, showing Saint Demetrius as a young *60* warrior, reveals the antique sources of the image. The frontal pose is not hieratic and the gaze fixed on the spectator is earnest and direct. With its long prominent nose, fleshy ears, low forehead, and large eyes with heavy eyelids, it could easily be a portrait of a real but perhaps everyday person, a contemporary of the painter. The melancholy expression of the mouth and eyebrows and the asymmetrical cast of the features reinforce the impression of life and verisimilitude. The modeling of the face is made more lifelike by the contrast of warm flesh tones and the green shadows, with a few white highlights emphasizing the salient features. In opposition to this manner, the costume, the armor, and the himation falling from the shoulder are treated much more conventionally. Their shapes and colors are primarily employed to emphasize the wealth of expression in the face. These traits, which can certainly be called realistic, connect the icon with the movement for renewal at the end of the thirteenth and beginning of the fourteenth centuries. In particular, the use of complementary colors and the curious shape of the ears recall the procedure of the Protaton painter. They are, however, not unlike the work of the painters Eutychios and Michael Astrapas in the Church of Peribleptos at Ohrid in 1295.

Another icon, Saint George, which is from the Monastery of Lavra and contemporary with *61* the icon from Vatopedi, is remarkable for the intense gaze of its close-set large eyes, under the heavy shadow of the beautifully drawn, continuous double-arch of the eyebrows. The narrow, dark shadow outlining the oval face and long nose contrasts with the broad planes of the flesh of the cheeks, forehead, and chin, which are flecked with red as if reflecting the vermilion mantle draped across the shoulders. The wealth of decorative elements — the martyr's crown, the pearl-trimmed borders of the gown, and the tight curls that wreathe the handsome face with its young Oriental features — seems to be a survival from the pictorial tradition of the twelfth century. But the intense expressiveness which gives the impression of a living presence belongs unquestionably to the beginning of the fourteenth century.

An icon of a warrior-saint at Mytilene follows the typical pattern for depicting such saints, *59* with abundant curls of hair framing a youthful face; but the personality portrayed is entirely different from that of the preceding warrior-saint in the Lavra icon. Delicate modeling, based especially on chiaroscuro and complementary colors, lends a quality of mingled tenderness and seriousness to the fragile features of the youth, just emerging from adolescence. Technically, the workmanship is much like that of a series of heads from the late thirteenth and early fourteenth centuries, which for the most part go back to the art of Constantinople. In more than one way the Saint George we have just considered is closely related to the beautiful head of Christ in the Monastery of Chilandar, usually dated around 1260.

74, 75   Yet another Saint George — an icon found at Aigion and restored for the Byzantine exhibition in 1964 — shows a further development of this type of portrait. With the passage of time there was a loss of that feeling for reality we noted previously in religious pictures as an essential factor and as an innovation. The approach here is much like that of the icon from Mytilene, but the total effect is more abstract and decorative. The asymmetrical face, its large eyes so close to the bridge of the nose, must be the result of an inexact copy of a model with the head turned slightly to one side. It has, nevertheless, a certain beauty; but it lacks that inner life which animates our other images of the same saint. We can mention the inorganic treatment of the hair, like a wig pushed down on the head, and the exaggerated emphasis on the concentric circles spreading across the armor. We must, of course, recognize the artist's desire for a decorative effect in the composition; this is based on the two circular motifs, the breastplate and the halo, of which the latter is decorated in relief work. It is difficult to say if this tendency toward the abstraction of everything ethical and human was a product of the development of art, or if it was the result of a provincial artist's attempt to copy a great work. In this case the latter seems more likely.

Such determined striving for faithful personification was not limited to saints of secondary importance, such as in the icons we have been considering; it also affected images of Christ and of the Virgin, which are usually less liable to variations in fashion. It is well known that of all the forms of Byzantine art these liturgical icons, which were usually placed on the iconostasis, were those most rigorously controlled by tradition. Nevertheless, a few icons of Christ or the Virgin from about 1300 prove that even these subjects were influenced, to a certain extent at least,

58   by the new ideas of the time. A Virgin and Child of the type known as Odegitria, in the Byzantine Museum at Athens, no longer shows the Virgin with the serene and dispassionate beauty found in such other images of the time as the Virgin Saviour of Souls in Ohrid, or in the Church of Chora (Kariye Cami) in Istanbul. Instead, she is here a mature woman with round, full cheeks, narrow, aquiline nose, prominent chin, and a small, melancholy mouth. Her general expression is in accord with that of her eyes, which gaze anxiously into space. The beautiful, aristocratic head with its quite individualized features is set on a graceful neck and framed by a gold-bordered, reddish-purple veil which falls in soft, rhythmic folds; and the contours above the forehead and at the base of the neck emphasize the length of the face. In its facial appearance, the icon most akin to this one is in the Tretyakov Gallery in Moscow, ascribed to Pimen, where the Virgin has the air of a great lady, at once severe and compassionate. But the Child in our picture, with its large head, high forehead, broad and full-fleshed face, and short, sturdy neck, comes from another tradition if not from another iconographic type. He is shown in three-quarter view in a rather uncomfortable posture; leaning slightly backward, His body and long rigid legs are tightly swaddled in the himation. He differs in this from the Child in a beautiful icon in the Hellenic Institute of Venice, who is more comfortably attired in a loose free-flowing garment in the antique manner. Moreover, the two figures in our icon do not show a homogeneous unity although the same technique is used for both — a technique much like that of the Saint Demetrius icon from Vatopedi.

53   Another icon of the Virgin in the Byzantine Museum at Athens shows a face with features so markedly individualistic, even disharmonious, that it borders on ugliness. The two sides of the face as well as the large eyes are asymmetrical in every detail. The contrast between the broad light surfaces of the apricot-colored skin and the greenish shadows is accentuated in order to

intensify the impression of relief. The plump face of the Child has the same characteristics. Such wholesome young faces, with frank, open gazes fixed on the viewer, were only possible in Byzantine painting around the year 1300, at which time a feeling developed for the realistic aspects of the personages depicted. One is inclined to ascribe this icon to the region of Salonica, at least until the center from which such tendencies were spread has been more convincingly localized. In any case, this type of Virgin gives an indication of the models for the Madonnas by Tuscan painters of the fourteenth century, which show very similar features.

This departure from the usual, classical ideal of beauty in Byzantine painting, occurring at a time when Hellenistic reminiscences were returning in strength, was probably due to a conscious opposition to the classicizing tendency, for it was a widespread phenomenon. The tendency may have been connected with the realistic trend of the period, or it may have been a real change in the concept of physical beauty, a question with regard to which these icons could be very instructive. The tendency extended to later periods, and finally culminated in a form of extreme expressionism in the popular art of the sixteenth and seventeenth centuries in Macedonia and the Epirus. Late in the fourteenth century, however, there was a tendency to revert to more abstract and beautiful faces as part of a general movement of return to a certain idealism.

In any event, in late fourteenth-century works one can still detect traces of those experiments conducted by previous generations. We see this, for example, in an icon depicting Christ with *70* donors, which is in Cyprus, although it was probably painted by an artist influenced directly by Constantinople: poorly preserved as it is, we can still admire its masterful execution. The drapery falls into a number of soft folds which are functional and, at the same time, extremely decorative in their graceful arabesques. This fine icon includes portraits of three actual individuals, one dead and two living: they are the girl for whose tomb it was made, together with her parents, the donors. These portraits of real people seem to have influenced the treatment of the face of Christ, for it is wider than the usual oval, and has prominent cheekbones, half-closed, slightly slanting eyes, and a narrow forehead. The face is neither realistic nor, as was the general rule, ideally beautiful; but neither can it be considered a portrait. For our purposes this work is the more significant because it bears a date: 1356.

An icon of Christ belonging to the Monastery of the Pantocrator on Mount Athos cannot be *71* far from this date. If we compare it with the icon of Christ Pantocrator in the Hermitage, Leningrad, which came from the same monastery and is dated 1363, we recognize the same type rendered with the same means but in a less linear manner. Characteristic of the workmanship of the Mount Athos icons are extremely fine and close brush strokes of light color which overlie other light-colored areas and lend translucency to the flesh tones. These groups of white, denser lines — the highlights — are disposed in such a way as to allow the modeling to emerge broadly and clearly. It must be added that although these lines are employed to compose the surfaces, the features are not outlined but take shape only through the use of light and shade; thus the beautiful countenance of the Christ Pantocrator appears bathed in a calm and gentle light. According to these conditions, this icon can be dated between 1350 and 1360. The high quality of its workmanship, as well as the nobility of the idealized face, point to the capital, Constantinople, as the place of origin.

The large and beautiful icon of the Archangel Michael in the Byzantine Museum, Athens, *64, 65* belongs to the same group. Since the youthful, beardless face is better preserved than in the icon previously discussed, we can more fully appreciate the fineness of the workmanship in the modeling through the play of light and shadow; the nose emerges strongly, and likewise the chin is made more prominent by the shadow on the neck. Unfortunately, we know from an icon of the Pantocrator from Zrza, near Prilep, dated 1394, that such lifelike rendering soon degenerated into a mechanical method of painting lights on the projecting sections. In our icon, the inscription on the globe, made up of the initials of Χριστὸς Δίκαιος Κριτής, "Christ the Righteous Judge," is typical of the image of Christ in the Great Deësis, itself a summary representation of the Last Judgment; thus it is likely that this icon was one of a series of five or seven icons of half-length figures which together made up a Great Deësis. One of the earliest examples is on the architrave from Vatopedi, described above, which must have decorated the top of an iconostasis. In point of fact, according to Simeon of Salonica, in the fourteenth century, "above, on the architrave, were the Saviour in the middle, and to either side of Him the Virgin and Saint John, angels, apostles, and other saints." A few such series are known; one is in the Tretyakov Gallery, Moscow, which came from Serbuchov but had been sent there from Constantinople toward the end of the fourteenth century; another is in the Monastery of Chilandar on Mount Athos; and there are still others. This arrangement of the iconostasis remained usual until the mid-sixteenth century. It then disappeared, surviving only in the architraves of small chapels or in isolated districts like Corfu, where the Great Deësis composed of fifteen separate icons was in use until the eighteenth century. In our icon, which must be dated about the third quarter of the fourteenth century, the characteristics of the portrait style are retained and the delicacy of the Virgin's face is combined with the candid earnestness of the face of a young man. This mixture is important in establishing the ideal of serene beauty of the human countenance and the lofty ethical values dominating the art of the capital at that time; it shows how capable was the art of that age to realize its high aims.

To follow some of the fluctuations in the sensitivity of fourteenth-century Byzantine painters, with regard to the human face and its spiritual aspect, we have examined a series of icons that represent busts of Christ, the Virgin, and some saints in the frontal position, that is, in the posture most nearly approaching the portraits painted in classical antiquity.

To round out this survey of portrait icons we must look at another category — the actual likenesses of real persons. There is no lack of these in mural paintings and in icons, for the donors of the work were often depicted. An icon of the Incredulity of Thomas from the Monastery of Meteora, recently published, is especially interesting from this standpoint because it can be dated and because portraits of real persons mingle unexpectedly here with the sacred personages. In it Christ is bending down before a closed door to expose the wound in His side; His arm is raised and His hand touches the head of a woman in ceremonial dress and another person, a man who is not one of the apostles. These have been identified as the Serbian princess, Maria Palaeologina, and her husband, Thomas Preljubović, Lord of Jannina (1361—84). This is the only known portrait of Thomas and is probably a true likeness, since he has an unpleasant appearance in accordance with his evil reputation as a Serbian despot. There are, however, two other portraits of the princess and we can, at least to some extent, check on the accuracy of this likeness. One is found on the wing of a diptych also commissioned by Maria Palaeologina in the same monastery; the other is on a copy of the complete diptych that is now in Cuenca, Spain. Although the figure of Maria is very small in all three cases, one can recognize the same features, and no attempt seems to have been made to flatter her. Especially in the icon of the Incredulity of Thomas this gentle female face with its expression of melancholy expectancy strikes a living note among the abstract faces of the apostles. While the work could have come from a workshop in Jannina, such workshops may well have included artists from other centers such as Salonica.

Other themes and other subjects were used for icons, and these themes provide invaluable insight into the representation of feelings such as suffering, pain, and grief as rendered by Byzantine painters in the second half of the fourteenth century.

The fine diptych in the Monastery of the Transfiguration at Meteora includes, on the right half, the dead Christ represented in accord with the type we have already seen in the small mosaic icon from Tatarna; on the left half is the Virgin, who contemplates her dead Son. Comparing these figures with the corresponding ones in the thirteenth-century Crucifixion and in the Tatarna mosaic icon, or with the Virgin in the Tretyakov Gallery which Lazarev dates in the thirteenth century, we see that the starkly dramatic contrasts have been softened in the later works. Consequently the general tone is milder despite the much more competent handling of details such as the close-knit eyebrows and the eyes. There dominates in the Meteora diptych an elegance of gesture and attitude that embodies the very different feelings of self-control and mute suffering. The noble countenance of Christ reveals even in death how His spirit did not crack under suffering. From the standpoint of technique, we find in the naked torso of Christ the same use of fine close lines to cover a surface which we noted in the faces of certain works discussed above. The analogies with the icon of the Crucifixion from Monemvasia remain valid, and the date cannot be later than the third quarter of the fourteenth century.

The famous Crucifixion in the Byzantine Museum, Athens, must be assigned to the same *55* period. The use of three figures was not new; in the earlier period it had been reserved, however, for monumental compositions without narrative details. In this case the composition appears to have monumentality principally because of the large Cross, and the three figures are isolated in space but linked in their common grief by a rhythmic movement flowing through each of them. What is new are the large, elongated figures whose height is emphasized by the low horizon line on which the simplified architecture of Jerusalem can be made out. The body of Christ is now only slightly bent, and the same curve is repeated in the figure of John, robust but harrowed with grief. The tall silhouette of the Virgin rises straight as a pillar, slender and aristocratic, wrapped in her great mantle. Her fragility introduces a lyrical note into the composition whose emotional elements, in any case, are extraordinarily restrained and free of excess. One scarcely notices that the three faces have been willfully disfigured by some barbarous hand. The somber colors seem muted by the diffuse light playing over the salient points of the bodies and draperies. This somberness determines the melancholy harmony of the entire composition, which resembles the Crucifixion at Daphni in its serene elegance.

In the same period, narrative composition was also changing in conformity with the spirit of the times. As it developed, numerous figures in movement were distributed throughout the depth of the picture plane and secondary scenes and incidents were included. A frequent subject during that period was the Miracle at Chonai; this can be studied in a fine icon from the Greek *69* Patriarchate of Jerusalem that was restored for the Byzantine exhibition of 1964 in Athens. The entire left half of the picture is filled by the impressive figure of the Archangel Michael in an energetic pose enlivened by *contrapposto;* the wings move in rhythm with the gestures and action of the body while the draperies flutter in the air. This impetuous yet elegant figure resembles that of another miracle-working angel in the frescoes of the Church of Chora (Kariye Cami), Istanbul, in which the angel drives away the Assyrians from the city of Jerusalem. The archangel in our icon retains the completely plastic fullness, the facial beauty, and the almost feminine hair-dressing of its presumed monumental prototype, but it becomes more impressive by contrast with the smallness of the figure of the monk Archippos. Here we recognize again the exploitation of contrast that was favored by the artists of the Palaeologue period.

Next to be considered is an icon of the Crucifixion from a church on the island of Patmos, *67* shown for the first time in the Byzantine exhibition of 1964 in Athens. The entire composition is in the form of a pyramid; the crucified Christ dominates from a rocky peak and the other personages are deployed along the two slopes. In the lower portion of the picture a small group dividing the garments of Christ forms a smaller triangle filling the space in front of the hill. Behind the Cross rise the walls and towers of Jerusalem against the gilded background. Despite its geometrical structure, the movement sweeps out in all directions, and the composition is still free enough to permit displacing the Cross from the middle ground to the rear, to allow room for the crowd of Jews. There are a few iconographic peculiarities: Saint John is placed near the Virgin (instead of on the opposite side of the Cross) in the same attitude of deep despair that we shall encounter again in the reliquary of Bessarion; the centurion is placed in front of and among the nine Jews; while his young comrades are not in military costume, and one of them, seen partly from the rear, makes a violent gesture challenging Jesus to descend from the Cross. The painter followed a prototype that incorporated various innovations, and can be dated about 1300. The coloring of the Patmos icon has a harmony of gray and ocher tones, of purplish red and dark violet; the vermilion tunic of the soldier crouching in the foreground, on the axis of the Cross, seems to underlie and intensify the entire chromatic scheme. The lighting, which is reinforced by the full modeling of the figures, is accentuated by white brush strokes that bring the figures into relief by outlining the folds of the draperies. This kind of modeling is familiar to us from the icon of the

73 Incredulity of Thomas from the Monastery of Meteora discussed above, and we shall encounter it many times again.

76 Another interesting example of the Crucifixion is represented on the cover of the reliquary which the Greek Cardinal Bessarion presented in 1463 to the Scuola della Carità in Venice; it later came to the Accademia of that city. The reliquary was unquestionably made in Constantinople. The Crucifixion is rigidly symmetrical, and composed of two groups: the Madonna with the Holy Women on one side of the Cross; Saint John, the Centurion, the sponge bearer, and the Jews on the other. The Christ on the Cross is fragile in physique but on a larger scale than the other figures, and His body is slightly twisted. At the foot of the rock three figures sit dividing up the cloak; one of them, as usual, is a soldier. The groups are arranged in depth like the entire composition, which moves from the trio dividing the cloak in the foreground to the fantastic walls of Jerusalem in the background. The remarkable, finely executed silhouettes of the various figures are elongated, slender, and weightless — thanks chiefly to the slight modeling, which is rendered by thin streaks of light on the flesh and by pale rivulets of lines on the gentle curves of the folds of garments. There are further reasons that place the work in the fourteenth century

73 after the Patmos icon, partly its relationship to the Incredulity of Thomas from Meteora, whose date is certain. This method of modeling, which reflects a gracious and idealistic spiritual attitude, has already been noted in the icons of Meteora and Patmos. It has a long history and was used especially in miniatures. In the fourteenth century it spread to icon painting and remained one of the most frequent methods well into the sixteenth and seventeenth centuries, as shall be

92, 93 seen when we examine the Descent into Limbo by Michael Damaskinos.

78, 79 An icon in the Benaki Museum, Athens, depicting the Hospitality of Abraham shows the ultimate point reached by these idealizing tendencies at the close of the century. While the pictorial space is very clear in the Patmos Crucifixion but already less in the Bessarion reliquary, it had always been employed most sparingly, and in this icon it loses much of its significance. The plane of the oval-shaped group of angels can scarcely be distinguished from that of the buildings in the background. Furthermore, the graceful figures have been rendered even more ethereal through the bright illumination and light brushwork. The decorative element has become more marked; the completely conventionalized architectural forms with their geometrical arrangement of verticals and horizontals serve to frame the willowy principal figures. The emphatic brightness of the picture serves as a foil for the narrow black patches of the doors and windows and the shimmer of light, pure colors. Through the radiance of these delicate colors, as well as the grace and elegance of the ethereal figures with their neutral faces, is here expressed the lyrical quality of a mystical religiousness that is in full accord with the theme of the picture, an Old Testament motif symbolizing the New Testament's Holy Trinity.

77 The same spiritual attitude is incorporated in an icon of the Archangel Michael in the Civic Museum of Pisa. There is an easy grace about the figure's pose and gesture despite its seeming monumentality; there are subtle harmonies of green and violet in the draperies; and there is fine

modeling, in which the white lines of the folds trace somewhat angular arabesques. All of these factors suggest that this icon should be dated about the end of the fourteenth century. The half-effaced inscription in Latin, the embossed frame with the arch, and its ornaments in the form of triangles in the corners, suggest a Western origin for this icon; but many of these traits are also found in a series of icons that are unquestionably Greek, in the monastery at Sinai.

Finally, an icon depicting the Baptism of Christ, from the Greek Patriarchate in Jerusalem, *81* proves that the approach to modeling was far from uniform at the end of the fourteenth century; it also shows that the graceful Hellenizing style, which had prevailed throughout the century, became more rigid at that time, and followed a geometrical tendency that was previously unknown in Byzantine art. The modeling perpetuates the manner we noted especially in works from the early part of the century which sought to bring out the plastic form of the body. But the light-streaked surfaces of these draperies, without losing their basic function, assume angular shapes; the nude body of Christ is anatomically almost perfect and has sharply defined shadows, while the rocks seem to have been cut out by scissors. As a result of this schematizing tendency, the poses are quite mannered — especially that of the Baptist. Two small figures in grisaille near the lower edge of the picture, who symbolize the Jordan and the sea, have the usual pictur-esqueness of accessory figures but they become, through their strictly symmetrical arrangement, relatively static supporting elements. Such traits are common in sculpture and miniatures from the end of the fourteenth and the beginning of the fifteenth centuries. Despite all these discrep-ancies, this icon remains a work of high quality.

In the development of icon painting, the frontier between the fourteenth and fifteenth centuries cannot always be traced clearly, and, therefore, many of the works we are about to consider may well belong to the end of the fourteenth century. There is, for example, a large liturgical icon in the Byzantine Museum, Athens, which portrays Saint Marina as a holy martyr, but the figure *83* retains all the nobility and stateliness of a great lady. Her draperies fall in slow rhythmic folds which broaden out in her ample hood. Such traits are typical of icons from the thirteenth and fourteenth centuries, as we have seen in the Saint James; but certain aspects lead us to date this *39* fine icon about 1400. The lack of plasticity in the red veil, the face that is disproportionately small in relation to the broad headcovering, and rather harshly modeled — these features recall in their technique the works of Theophanus the Greek in Russia, about 1405, and in their solidity the angel in the Great Deësis at Chilandar, after 1400.

On a double-sided icon in Mytilene, Christ occupies one face and John the Evangelist the *87* other. The great bulk of Saint John bursts beyond the limits of the frame; his huge head shows a wild expression, and his powerful hands hold a large, open Gospel. The modeling, through its vigorous contrasts, brings the head into strong relief, and the drapery has massive folds. This sculpturesque and far from spiritual figure was derived from the fiery old men painted by Manuel Panselinos on the walls of the Protaton, or by Eutychios and Michael Astrapas, in the Peribleptos at Ohrid, around 1300. What leads us to date the icon after 1400 is a certain stiffness in the dra-peries, the similarity of its forms to those of the apostle in the Deësis at Chilandar (though the latter is much calmer), and, finally, the related manner of its modeling in comparison with certain figures done in 1428 in the Pantanassa Monastery at Mistra.

It must be recognized that such a regression to models of a school which, to all intents and purposes, had been extinct for three generations is not an isolated phenomenon. There is, for example, a triptych in the Benaki Museum showing the Virgin and Child on the central panel *86* and a saint on either wing. The broad modeling, the wrathful expression of the Child, and such details as the shape of the ears remind us of icons from the beginning of the fourteenth century. Other traits, such as the delicate workmanship and vivid coloring, make us assign this icon to the second half of the fifteenth century.

85   An icon of the Dormition of the Virgin from the Monastery of Saint John on Patmos brings us to another aspect of icon painting in the fifteenth century, namely, the influences exerted by

47, 49   Italian art. Thirteenth-century icons, as we have explained, reveal certain direct consequences of the immediate contact with Western art, especially during the French occupation. In the fourteenth century, however, Western influences definitely abated, even in regions occupied by the Venetians and other "Franks." But in the fifteenth century signs of a certain influence of the West upon the East crop up more frequently. As a result of the narrow frame of the Patmos icon, its composition is typically simplified, and dominated by the tall, elongated figure of Christ which stands out in front of a mandorla surmounted by a seraph. Everything in this icon is Byzantine except the two buildings; the peaked roofs with rose windows in the pediments and, above all, the perspective treatment clearly betray their debt to Giotto.

88, 89   This survey of fifteenth-century icons can be concluded with a remarkable work from the Byzantine Museum at Athens which was brought from Asia Minor during the last exodus of the Greek population in 1922. It contains an illustration of the Magnificat, combined with a multitude of small scenes crowded with figures. Such a profusion of small figures within a miniature format is most unusual in Byzantine icons. The postures and faces of these tiny personages are often brimming with life, and although some are naïve, they are always masterfully rendered. It is difficult to assign this work to a particular center, but one on the lower left shows the donor, a monk, kneeling before the Virgin and Child, and a chapel behind has a rose window in its façade. Would it be too daring to suppose that this icon was painted in a region where chapels had such occidental rose windows? This was the case in Crete, and there are no factors in this icon to rule out that origin.

    The sixteenth century perpetuated the traditions of the preceding periods with a fidelity that may sometimes confuse even the specialists. The artistic center was shifted to Crete, and to the island came painters from Constantinople, such as Alexios Apokavkos in 1421 and Nicholas Philanthropinos in 1419; and others came from Mistra, including Xenos Dighenis in 1461; all brought with them the styles of the great centers. This explains the purity of the iconography and style in sixteenth-century Cretan painting which made it the quasi-official school of painting for the Orthodox Church. The best features of this mid-sixteenth-century art are apparent in the

96   icon of the Nativity, now in the Hellenic Institute of Venice. It has taken over with scrupulous fidelity from some prototype of the Palaeologue period, such as the Church of the Peribleptos at Mistra, the richness of the landscape composition, the stratification of planes, and the pictorial motifs, as well as the soft modeling and the measured grace of the poses. But the composition has become calmer and more symmetrical in the sixteenth-century icon; the arrangement of the draperies is now subordinated to a geometrical rhythm, and the mountains are more severely stylized. Moreover, accessory elements borrowed from Italian art are discreetly introduced here and there — the rabbit and doe remind us of Pisanello. The manger is correctly rendered in perspective and chiaroscuro.

91   But most of the scenes are untouched by any Italian influence: for example, the Descent from the Cross painted on the border of an icon of the Virgin now in the Benaki Museum at Athens. This firm composition with its elongated figures full of nobility and restraint could be enlarged to the dimensions of a mural painting without the slightest change. And we find, in fact, the same severe, sober style and the same masterly workmanship in the frescoes done in the mid-sixteenth century by Cretan painters on Mount Athos, or in the monasteries of Meteora.

    At times one has the impression that an artist was striving to return to the forms of the fourteenth and fifteenth centuries, as in certain icons by Michael Damaskinos, the outstanding Cretan

92, 93   painter of the second half of the sixteenth century — notably in the Descent into Limbo that bears his signature, in the Benaki Museum at Athens. The transparent coloring and delicate brushwork in the modeling of the figures, which are at once grave and ethereal, remind us strongly of the fourteenth-century icons we have discussed.

Sixteenth-century icons with single figures retain and, indeed, reinforce the monumental sculpturesque feeling which, although weakened in form, had been handed down from the fourteenth and fifteenth centuries. The icon of Saint John the Evangelist from Patmos repeats the type that *94* was current in the fourteenth century, in which he is depicted as a writer with his inkhorn clasped under his arm. The figure fills the entire pictorial field; the powerful head with its exaggerated brow is inclined to one side in grief, but the bulk of the body seems nonexistent beneath a mass of draperies. Highlights outline the drapery folds in straight-edged triangles with no hint of a curve; this peculiarity is common to icons by the painter Euphrosynos, dating from 1542, and to a number of other Cretan icons from the mid-sixteenth century. This conservative spirit was carried over into the seventeenth century, as we see in the large icon in the Benaki Museum signed by Emmanuel Tzane in 1637. This youthful work shows Saint Anne with the Virgin holding a *95* flower as a symbol of Christ. The outstanding Cretan artist succeeded in retaining not only the impeccable technique of the great tradition but also the expression of serene majesty and austere tenderness. These qualities have always, from time immemorial, constituted the great glory of Byzantine painting.

37 RAISING OF LAZARUS. 12th-13th centuries. 8¹/₂×9¹/₂″. Private collection, Athens

39 SAINT JAMES. 13th century. 35⁷/₈ × 25⁵/₈″. Monastery of Saint John the Evangelist, Patmos

41 SAINT PETER. 12th century. The Protaton, Mount Athos

42 SAINT PANTELEIMON. 12th century. 15¹/₈×10″. Monastery of Lavra, Mount Athos

43 CHRIST PANTOCRATOR. 12th century. Detail of an icon on the architrave of an iconostasis. Dimensions of entire panel, 27¹/₈×83⁷/₈″. Monastery of Vatopedi, Mount Athos

44 CRUCIFIED CHRIST. Detail, plate 45

45 CRUCIFIXION. 13th century. Double-faced icon. 34¹/₄×24¹/₄″. Byzantine Museum, Athens

46 THE APOSTLE JOHN. Detail, plate 45

47 VIRGIN. 13th century. Detail of a Crucifixion, on a double-faced icon. Dimensions of entire icon, 38¹/₄×31⁷/₈″. Palace of the Archbishop, Nicosia, Cyprus

48 CHRISTUS IMAGO PIETATIS (THE DEAD CHRIST). Beginning of 14th century. Mosaic. Dimensions without frame, 6⁷/₈×5¹/₈″. Monastery of Tatarna, Eurytania

49 SAINT GEORGE. 13th century. Double-faced icon in painted relief. 42⁷/₈×28³/₈″. Byzantine Museum, Athens

51 VIRGIN "EPISKEPSIS." 14th century. Mosaic. 37³/₈×24³/₈″. Collection of the Refugees from Asia Minor, Byzantine Museum, Athens

53 VIRGIN AND CHILD. 14th century. 32⁵/₈×22⁷/₈″. Collection of the Refugees from Asia Minor, Byzantine Museum, Athens

55 CRUCIFIXION. 14th century. Double-faced icon. 40¹/₂×33¹/₈″. Byzantine Museum, Athens

57 SAINT NICHOLAS. Beginning of 14th century. Mosaic. 16³/₄×13³/₈″. Monastery of Stavronikita, Mount Athos

58 VIRGIN AND CHILD. 14th century. 33¹/₂×25⁵/₈″. Byzantine Museum, Athens

59 WARRIOR-SAINT. Detail. 13th-14th centuries. Dimensions of entire panel, 36³/₄×28¹/₂″. Palace of the Archbishop, Mytilene

60 SAINT DEMETRIUS. 14th century. 34⁵/₈×20¹/₂″. Monastery of Vatopedi, Mount Athos

61 SAINT GEORGE. 14th century. 28¹/₂×18⁷/₈″. Monastery of Lavra, Mount Athos

62 MATER DOLOROSA. End of 14th century. Wing of a diptych (see plate 63). 10⁵/₈×8¹/₄″. Monastery of the Transfiguration, Meteora

63 THE CRUCIFIED CHRIST. End of 14th century. Wing of a diptych (see plate 62). 8⁵/₈×7¹/₂″. Monastery of the Transfiguration, Meteora

64 HEAD OF THE ARCHANGEL MICHAEL. Detail, plate 65

65 THE ARCHANGEL MICHAEL. 14th century. 43¹/₄× 32¹/₈″. Byzantine Museum, Athens

67 CRUCIFIXION. 14th century. 13¹/₄×10¹/₂″. Chapel of the Annunciation, Patmos

69 MIRACLE AT CHONAE. 14th century. 16³/₄×14¹/₈″. Greek Patriarchate, Jerusalem

70 CHRIST PANTOCRATOR. Dated 1356, by the dedication. Detail. Dimensions of entire icon, 99¹/₄×16⁷/₈″. Palace of the Archbishop, Nicosia, Cyprus

71 CHRIST PANTOCRATOR. 14th century. Double-faced icon. 40³/₄×28″. Monastery of the Pantocrator, Mount Athos

39

41

44

46

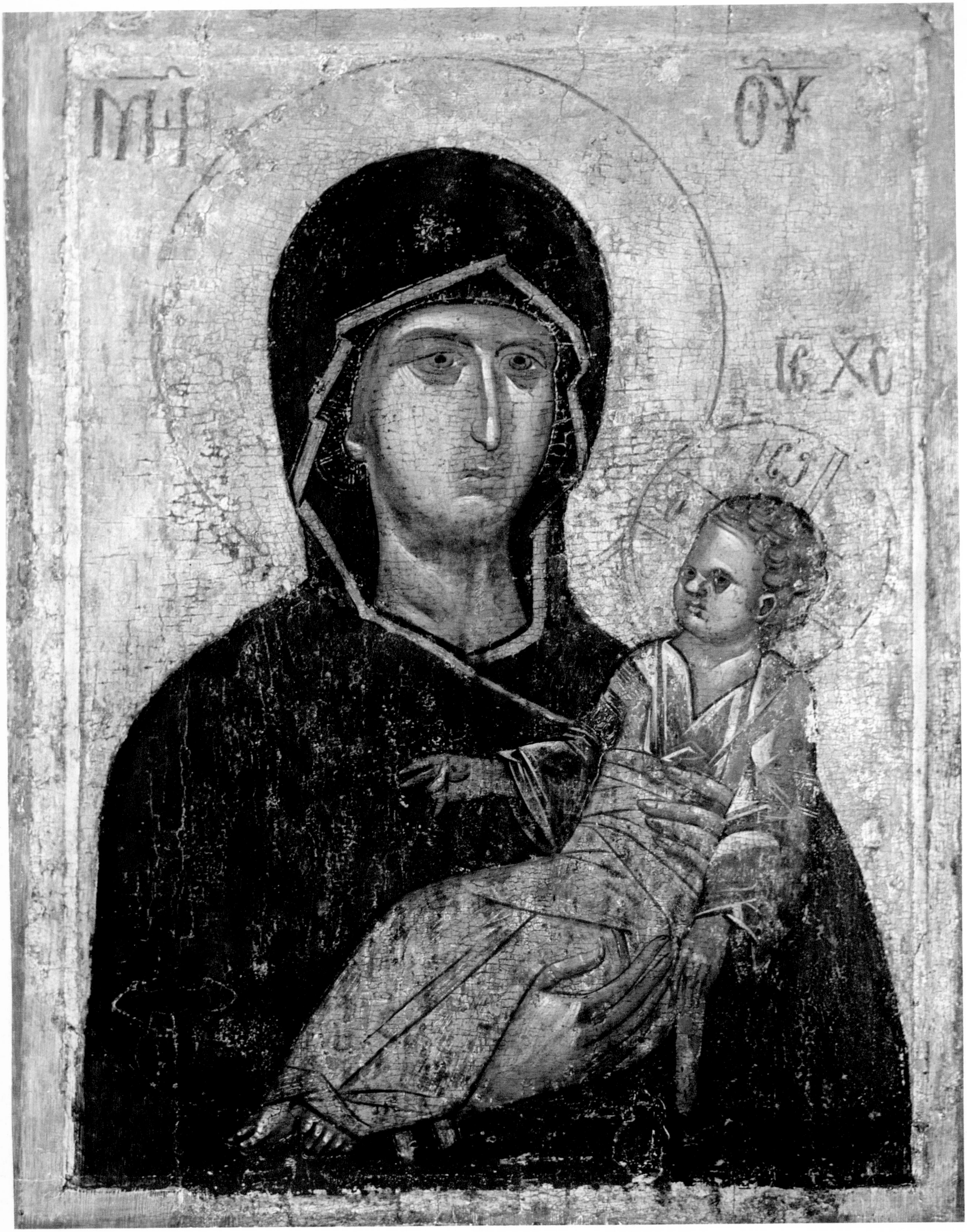
ΘΥ
IC XC

72

76

MAR   NA

83

94

ΗΑΑ   ΝΝΑ

ΜΡ ΘΥ

95

III. BULGARIA

Icon Painting from the Ninth to the Seventeenth Century *by Krsto Miatev*

Plates 97—156

It is not known when the icon first became an object of religious devotion in the central part of the Balkan peninsula, but it may have been as early as the middle of the first millennium of the Christian era. By that time conditions were ripe for it. Christianity had penetrated the area with its rituals and its art in the fourth century. The fact that this region was politically dependent on the Eastern Roman Empire and situated near Constantinople and the other Christian centers in Asia Minor, Syria, and Palestine had a decisive effect on the first Christian congregations in this part of the Balkan peninsula, both in the content and character of its rites and art. Thus, when the earliest Christian icons were produced in its communities, they closely conformed to the old Hellenistic tradition of portraiture. Unfortunately, no such portrait icons have come down to us, nor do early religious writers make any mention of icons in that region. A few frescoes have survived, and they shed some light on early Christian painting in the Balkans — as well as, indirectly, on what the first Bulgarian icons must have been like.

Paintings that have been discovered on the ceilings and walls of a few burial chambers in the necropolis of Serdika (present-day Sofia) date from the fourth to sixth centuries. These frescoes consist mainly of decorative and symbolic motifs; but on the spandrels of the vault in one burial crypt, which was decorated in the fifth century, are half-length figures (without haloes) of the Archangels Michael, Gabriel, Uriel, and Raphael. In style and technique they undeniably recall the impressionistic portrait icons of Ancient Greece.[1]

In the same period, monumental churches were built in many places in Bulgaria; some were decorated with frescoes and mosaic floors. One of these, known as the "Red Church," located near the village of Peruštice in the district of Plovdiv, still has fragments of large-scale frescoes from the seventh century. Not only are there Biblical scenes, but also round medallions with busts of winged females depicted as portraits and resembling the busts in the medallions in Bawit.[2]

Both examples demonstrate that the earliest Christian art in the Balkans borrowed its subject matter, iconography, and style from Palestine, Syria, Egypt, and Asia Minor, where Hellenistic traditions were still in force and the deeds of the first Christian martyrs had not been forgotten. For those reasons it was there, too, that the first Christian icons were created. From the eastern provinces of the Byzantine Empire, icons, together with their cult and their iconographic and stylistic peculiarities, made their way to Constantinople, the capital of secular and spiritual authority. There, especially after 843 when the reverence of icons had become an established part of the religion, the icon reached its richest development as a significant branch of Byzantine art.

In the earliest phase of development of Christian icons in the Balkans, an important political event occurred. In 681, a part of the Byzantine Balkans was formed into the first Bulgarian state. It is quite certain that the period of non-Christian domination in the new state, between 681 and 865, was anything but favorably disposed toward the preservation and further development of religious art. However, things changed with the official conversion to Christianity in 865, and this in itself helped unite the Slavs into the now expanded Bulgarian state. Inevitably, the political ties of the time impelled the Bulgarian court to take over bodily the new religion and the entire church apparatus from Constantinople, along with its theological literature, religious music, and painting. Boris (852—89), the first Christian prince in Bulgaria, quickly built seven cathedrals in various parts of his kingdom. His successors, Simeon (893—927) and Peter (927—69), in cooperation with the nobility and clergy, carried on his efforts and built more churches and a number of monasteries which soon became centers of literary and artistic activity.

In the tenth century, the Bulgarian state attained its highest political and cultural development. Its territories spread in the north from the Danube to the Carpathians and southern Hungary, and reached the Adriatic in the southwest. Bulgaria bordered on Byzantium on the south and maintained close political, economic, and cultural ties. In this respect the two chief Byzantine cities, Constantinople and Salonica, played a most important role. After a Slavic alphabet had been devised, native writers in the chief city of Bulgaria produced a rich and, for the time, unusual literature of original works in the native language, as well as translations, and many of these manuscripts were enhanced by miniatures. Archaeologists have unearthed the vestiges of numerous churches of the ninth and tenth centuries which have a variety of architectural forms: basilicas, cruciform churches, and tri-apsidal (treifoil-plan) churches with cupolas. One of these, in Preslav, was of a round design unusual for the time and was adorned outside and inside with rich and diversified plastic decoration. Its walls were covered with costly marbles as well as mosaics on a gold ground; these ornaments were further enhanced, like its altars and pulpits, by polychrome ceramics with geometrical and floral motifs which imitated the enamel plaques in the churches of Constantinople.[3] According to John Exarchos, a Bulgarian writer of the early tenth century, the dwellings of the Preslav boyars were decorated on the outside with marble, wood, and paint, and the church interiors shone with gold and silver.[4] Furthermore, churches and palaces of the time were ornamented with the first frescoes in Bulgaria on religious themes, like those which must certainly have existed, after the conversion to Christianity, in the first Bulgarian capital, Pliska.

No doubt the icon also took its place in the first Bulgarian churches and in everyday life once its cult had been solemnly authorized after long controversy and persecution. This authorization occurred in 843, only twenty-two years after the Bulgarian royal court had accepted conversion to Christianity. The first icons to appear there after the official conversion must certainly have been brought in from the Byzantine capital and eastern provinces, but most of them probably came from Jerusalem, which promptly became the goal of Bulgarian pilgrims. The Bulgarians quickly assimilated both the subject matter and the style of these icons from abroad.

The early literature of Bulgaria tells us that icons existed there in the tenth century, and even before. John Exarchos, who lived and worked in Preslav in the late ninth and early tenth centuries, was undoubtedly aware of the movement in Byzantium which opposed the use of religious images. Lest such iconoclastic conceptions and attitudes make headway among the newly Christianized Bulgarians, John translated into the native tongue forty-eight of the one hundred chapters of the book by John of Damascus, *Of Icons, That Is, of Images*.[5]

At the end of the tenth century an ardent defense for the use of icons in worship appeared in the *Sermon against the Bogomils* by Presbyter Cosmas. Like John Exarchos, he supported his views by citing the ruling of the Nicene Council of 787, that the cult of icons is not idolatry since it is not the icon as a material object which is revered but rather the personage — "depicted true to himself, whether young or old" — who is represented.[6] From Presbyter Cosmas we also learn something of the subjects in Bulgarian icons of the tenth century. He mentions icons of Christ, the Virgin, and various saints ("whoever fails to kiss with love and awe the icons of Our Lord or His Mother and all the Saints, may be damned! . . . And when we behold on an icon the blessed Mother of God, then we cry out from the very depths of our hearts: Most Holy Mother of God, forget not thy children! . . . But when we true believers behold the image of God portrayed on an icon, then we stretch out our hands to Him").

Cosmas also speaks of the especially beloved type of depiction of the Virgin, the so-called Odegitria type: "When we behold on an icon His lovable image clasped in thine arms, then do we sinners rejoice, sink to our knees, and kiss Him with adoration." There were, in addition, icons of individual saints: "But when we behold a saint portrayed, then do we say: 'Saint of God, pray for me, so that I may find my salvation through my prayers!'" From the same writer we learn finally that icons were painted in color on wooden panels: "The evil spirits quake in fear before the image of the Lord painted on a board. . . . We do not bow before either the paint or the wood, but rather before Him who is portrayed thereon." An icon of the Odegitria Virgin is mentioned by the Byzantine historiographer, Leo the Deacon, as having been in the palace or the palace church in Preslav until 972. After the sack of the Bulgarian capital by Emperor Jon Tsimiskes, this icon was transported with all due solemnity to Constantinople as a trophy of war.[7]

The Orthodox icons described by Presbyter Cosmas and Leo the Deacon were probably not all brought into Bulgaria from Constantinople; some were turned out by native icon painters. It is certain, however, that they were of the same high artistic quality as the icons created in the Byzantine capital.

Of all the icons of Preslav, only one has survived. It dates from around 900, about thirty years after the official conversion of Bulgaria,[8] and was discovered in fragments among the ruins of the Monastery of Patlejna near Preslav. This icon is an exception, being painted not on wood but, instead, on several separate plaques of light yellow clay which were mounted on a wall. It portrayed Saint Theodore in life size, and the few vestiges of this icon which have been found show that the Eastern iconography of this saint had been retained in Bulgaria — an ascetic face with a long, pointed beard and thin, drooping moustache. The contours are bold but there is little modeling of the features. Many other archaeological finds in Preslav prove that such icons, painted on rectangular or round plaques of baked clay, large or small, were no rarity in the Bulgarian capital in the tenth century. There can be no doubt that icons of wood or enamel served as models for these ceramic icons; although the prototypes were usually Byzantine, Slavic inscriptions have been found on many of the ceramic fragments in Preslav.

The Golden Age of the Bulgarian state and its culture lasted until 1018, when the country was finally conquered by Byzantium and robbed of its own administration and national church. Under Byzantine rule, only a few new religious edifices were built and decorated with frescoes and icons; among them are the monastery of Bačkovo with its two-storied crypt, the church of the Asens in the fortress near Asenovgrad, Saint George in Sofia, and the old Church of Saint Nicholas. Some of the frescoes have survived to the present day, but the icons were not preserved — or have not, at any rate, come to light. We know that there were Byzantine icons in Bulgaria in the twelfth century from a Greek epigram by Theodore Valsamon, entitled "On the Saint Demetrius Discovered by the Emperor in the House of Slavopeter the Rebel." According to this epigram, the Byzantine Emperor Isaac II Angelus, during his campaign against the rebellious Bulgarians in 1186, found in a fortress north of Stara Planina (perhaps the capital city of Tirnovo) an icon of Saint Demetrius that had been spirited away from Salonica. The icon must have been highly prized, for its recovery caused great rejoicing among the Byzantines and the Emperor gave orders that a protective cover should be made of precious metals.[9]

After the successful uprising of 1185, the Bulgarians re-established their national state with Tirnovo as the capital. Under Tsar Ivan Asen (1218—41) Bulgaria's borders stretched once again to three seas, and in the thirteenth and fourteenth centuries literature, architecture, and art flourished once more. Writers and painters turned out works of importance, both secular and sacred, with miniatures, vignettes, and decorative initials embellishing their manuscripts. In the frescoes which survive in many old churches, we can still see what a high level of achievement such large-scale painting reached. The artists who painted frescoes and miniatures were certainly icon painters as well, since monumental painting and icon painting have always gone hand in hand. Mural art lent its subjects, iconographic schemes, and stylistic approaches to icons, and in return the icons furnished new iconographic models to the mural paintings.

In the mid-twelfth century, the artist who decorated the crypt-church of Bačkovo painted busts of archbishops in the apse and crypt; these were in round or rectangular illusionistic frames, making it appear as if the frescoes consisted of pictures hanging on the wall. In doing this, he perpetuated in Bulgaria the Hellenistic tradition of painted portraits although, in this case, the portraits take on the characteristics of icons.[10] In the course of the thirteenth and fourteenth centuries, Bulgarian fresco artists borrowed still other motifs typical of icons. Examples of this are: the Three Mothers — Elisabeth, Anne, and Mary, shown nursing their children — in the frescoed lunette over the entrance door of the Church of the Forty Martyrs in Tirnovo, that dates from 1230;[11] in the Acheiropoietos — the miraculously painted image — of the Virgin in the lunette over the door of the church in Bojana from 1259;[12] and in the Virgin Odegitria in the lunette over the entrance to the ossuary in Bačkovo from about 1343.[13] A typical iconic composition is also found in the lunette over the west door of the church in the Dragalevci monastery, which was done at the end of the fifteenth century. Here the Virgin is depicted with the Child on her lap, both figures presented frontally. To either side are the Archangels Michael and Gabriel, both bowing deeply, and behind the throne stand two other angels.[14]

Sometimes, especially in smaller churches in the thirteenth and fourteenth centuries, the large icons that were normally set up on either side of the altar partition were replaced by copies in fresco. Thus, the enthroned Christ Evergetos and the standing figure of Saint Nicholas on either side of the altar area in the church in Bojana, from 1259, are undoubtedly substitutes for icons of which one, that with Christ, certainly must have come from Constantinople.[15] This practice was continued during the fourteenth and fifteenth centuries. On the south wall of the fourteenth-century church in the village of Berenda, one finds, directly next to the iconostasis, a monumental Saint Peter painted in fresco as a bust in frontal position. It is twice the size of the other pictures of saints in the church, and this bust also differs from the others in that it is enclosed in a frame which likewise is in fresco.[16]

A hundred years later, a copy was similarly made of the altar icon of Saint Demetrius in the Monastery of Saint Demetrius in the village of Boboševo. Here, too, the frescoed icon is on the wall directly next to the iconostasis and here, too, the portrait of the saint is surrounded by a frescoed frame, different from all the other frescoes in the church.[17]

The originals of these thirteenth- and fourteenth-century icons have not been preserved in Bulgaria but they must have existed and the frescoed copies are our best guide to distinguishing their various iconographic types. The close relationship between the icons and the copies in fresco is borne out by certain wall paintings from the fifteenth and sixteenth centuries, since we do have icons from that time with motifs that were directly and faithfully taken over into the fresco copies. The best known of these are the icons of Saint George and of Saint Demetrius, astride their fiery steeds; the saints are in one case slaying a dragon, and in the other the enemy is being trampled under horse's hoofs. The same compositions were painted on the walls of the Dragalevci and Kremikovci monasteries at the end of the fifteenth century.[18] The miracle of Saint George is represented in the same way in both monasteries: George is piercing the dragon with his lance, thus rescuing the princess, who stands before the ramparts from which spectators are watching the hero's exploit. At Dragalevci, there are two scenes with warrior-saints on horseback: on one, Saint Demetrius, named "Great Prince" on the inscription of the fresco, just as on the icon; on the other, Saint Mercurius, his naked sword in hand, triumphs over Julian the Apostate.[19]

The lunette of Saint George over the entrance in the vestibule of the monastery of Kremikovci is likewise a copy of an icon. The saint sits on a backless throne with a long spear in his right hand. He is dressed as an armored knight with the head of Medusa on his breastplate and the slain dragon at his feet.[20]

All available evidence shows that during the thirteenth and fourteenth centuries icons were widely diffused throughout Bulgaria. During the entire period their subject matter, iconography, and style were intimately related to those of fresco painting in the neighboring countries, especially Byzantium whose icons were highly appreciated, much sought after, and widely copied. Because the neighboring peoples shared the same religion, icons were easily distributed from one country to another with no frontiers or political opposition to hinder their exchange.

A well-known Bulgarian icon, known in the literature as "la Sainte Face de Laon," was first sent to Rome and then, in 1249, to the Cathedral of Laon in northern France near the present Belgian border.[21] This icon shows the face of Christ as miraculously imprinted on the Cloth of Veronica, the mandilion. The motif arose in Byzantium within the ninth to eleventh centuries and became widely diffused throughout Christendom, both East and West. Here, the face of Christ is painted in dark brown tones and framed by luxuriant hair and a pointed beard. It stands out sharply from the taut linen which is patterned in latticework and a lily motif. The image is very close to the classical Byzantine depiction of Christ; both Hellenistic illusionism and the twelfth-century Byzantine technique of miniature painting are recalled by the drawing and the manner of painting — the de-emphasis of outlines, the delicate nuances in tone, and the subtle modeling of the flesh. Yet this icon did not originate in Constantinople, but was painted by a Slavic artist who was very familiar with the iconography and style of Byzantine painting of the time. The inscription in Middle Bulgarian and the orthography show clearly that it must have been done at the beginning of the thirteenth century in the Bulgarian capital of Tirnovo. The peregrination of this icon from Bulgaria to France was by no means an isolated case; Bulgarian icons were much sought after in Russia and the neighboring countries.[22]

Fine icons, whether originals or copies, were esteemed as pious and valuable gifts. Icons often bore the name of the church or monastery where their original was to be found, even when the designation did not, in fact, correspond to the iconographic type depicted. The famous icon of the Virgin in the monastery of Bačkovo came from Constantinople or from Georgia, according to the inscription on its silver casing. The picture itself has become so blackened through time that little more than its general contours can be made out. It cannot be compared with any of the single-figure compositions of the Virgin of the Vlaherniotis type, but only with the well-known type of the Virgin Eleousa. One can still make out the figure of the Virgin, closely resembling the Odegitria type, and the Child embracing His mother and resting His head against her face. The background, haloes, and part of the frame are hidden by the silver casing which, as was customary in the fourteenth century, is richly decorated and has a long inscription in Georgian stating that the icon was donated to the monastery in 1310 by two brothers of that country.[23] A similar icon of the Odegitria type is now erroneously described on the silver case as "Eleousa" because, in *107* 1342, it was donated by a close relative of Tsar Ivan Alexander to the Monastery of the Virgin Eleousa in Nessebri.[24] This icon, however, is no longer of importance as an example of painting because, in the course of a restoration during the sixteenth and seventeenth centuries, both the faces and the drapery were much repainted in the calligraphic style favored at that time.

Among the outstanding icons of the late fourteenth century, a splendid double-sided example *102, 103, 105* must not be overlooked. It was presented to the Monastery of John the Evangelist near the village of Poganovo by the Byzantine Empress Helena, who was the wife of Emperor Manuel II Palaeologue, the daughter of the local Prince Constantine Dejanov, and the granddaughter of Tsar Ivan Alexander.[25] This rich gift to a small monastery was not without cause: before her marriage the Empress and her father had founded this monastery and when, in 1395, he fell in the battle with the Turks in Wallachia, she presented the monastery with this costly icon. On the front side are depicted the Virgin and the patron saint of the monastery, Saint John the Evangelist. On the back is a copy of the mosaic "The Miracle in the Monastery of Christ Latom," in the apse of the Church of Christ Latom in Salonica. The Virgin and Saint John have elongated, continuous, unbroken silhouettes turned slightly to right and left, and the graceful inclination of the heads toward one another serves to unite the two figures. The quiet repose of the figures, the gentle bending of the heads, and the facial expressions all make for an atmosphere of restrained grief. The exceptional care given to finishing every detail, the warm modeling of the flesh, and the elegant draping of the garments must be due to a great master, an exponent of the Palaeologue style at its most mature stage. The figure of the Virgin has a close analogy to that in another double-sided icon of the fourteenth century that is now in the Byzantine Museum at Athens where it is ascribed to a master from Salonica.[26]

99   Related to this icon from Constantinople is one from Nessebri depicting the Virgin of the Eleousa type.[27] This is also from the fourteenth century and has the same emotional quality. The Virgin and Child are locked in a gentle embrace and the Child, brimming with innocent happiness, snuggles close to the mother and rests His head against her cheek. The happy mood and trustful nature of the Child contrast with the inward peace and dreamy pensiveness of the mother, who bends her head forward slightly to meet the Infant's caress. An almost imperceptible smile hovers about her mouth, but her gaze, heavy with grim foreboding of the tragic destiny of the Child in her arms, is directed far beyond the picture. A deep human feeling is brought out in the intimate relationship of the figures, their expressions and gestures, and the warm coloring of their garments; in this respect the icon from Nessebri comes close to Italian madonnas of the fifteenth century.

We can cite only a few examples of icons presented as gifts by persons in high positions; in the following centuries, however, innumerable instances are known for the faithful placed unlimited trust in the efficacy of such gifts to win salvation for themselves. Yet, of the abundant treasure of art which once existed, very little has come down to us; between 1396, when Bulgaria fell to the Turks, and 1878 the political life, economy, and religion of the country were those of an appendage to the Ottoman Empire. In the invaded country, hundreds of churches were looted and burned to the ground and others were converted into mosques. Where, by chance, a church was spared, its icons lay hidden away for centuries in damp rooms and, even now, many have not been cleaned or studied. In the absence of new icons, unskillful painters "restored" old ones that were damaged and dirty by repainting them clumsily. In many cases, superstitious monks and priests burned old icons which were no longer in use, believing that these holy objects could be rescued from sacrilege only by fire.

Somewhat more favorable conditions for the development of Bulgarian icons did not set in until the seventeenth century, when the Turkish overlords finally authorized the Bulgarians to build new churches. Although the outside of these ordinary-looking single-nave churches had nothing in particular to recommend them as architecture, their interiors were richly decorated with frescoes on walls and vaults, and the gilded iconostases gleamed with icons. The first Bulgarian historian, Pajsije, who wrote his *Slavic Bulgarian History* in 1762, in the monastery of Chilandar, mentions a monk named Pimen: he had learned architecture and painting in the monasteries on Mount Athos and, in the first half of the seventeenth century, was very active in those two fields in the bishopric of Sofia. According to Pajsije, Pimen was also a highly skilled painter of icons.[28] Obviously, the work of the monk from Athos was not an isolated instance, for in the seventeenth century many new churches were erected in towns, villages, and monasteries in other regions of the country, and these were decorated with frescoes and new icons. As far as we now know, the most important centers of icon painting were certain monasteries on Mount

Athos and, in Bulgaria, the monastery of Etropole and the cities of Tirnovo, Sofia, Nessebri, and Vraca. Many icons were enhanced by new decorative elements, such as embossed aureoles, and carved frames which sometimes surrounded the entire icon or only the central figure. No other firsthand literary sources tell us about this revival of architecture and icon painting in Bulgaria, but we know that there actually was a revival from the relatively large number of churches, frescoes, and icons that have survived from the seventeenth century.

Artists in the past were unfortunately not in the habit of signing their works, and thus we know little about them. The earliest signed icons known in Bulgaria date only from the seventeenth century; from these we can gather the following names, among others: Yerey Gergin (1642), Nedelko the Painter (1652), Stamen the Painter (1667), Vassili the Monk (1667), the parish priest Peter, Lord of Toma (1699), Nicholas (1703), the teachers Kosta and Tson (1750), Panaiot the Painter (1715), and Thomas Vishanov (end of the eighteenth century). Many of the signatures are in Greek, but this is no proof that the artists were Greek, for under Byzantine and then under Turkish rule the Bulgarian church was a dependency of the Constantinople patriarchate and Greek was its official ecclesiastical language. *133, 135*

The Bulgarian icon painters of the seventeenth and eighteenth centuries faithfully carried on the old iconographic traditions. They respected the time-honored basic schemes and employed old handwritten manuals as guides, the so-called Erminiji. This did not prevent them from borrowing sundry Baroque and Rococo motifs from the West for ornamental decoration and for certain iconographic details. Thus, for example, in an icon of the Nativity the traditional Byzantine composition of the Virgin and Joseph is completely altered into a Western configuration; both of them kneel in adoration in the cave on either side of the crib where the Christ Child lies. *155*

The great demand in Bulgaria for icons, from the eighteenth century on, encouraged the rise of a popular folk-style in icon art. Monks, priests, and local teachers lacking professional training made clumsy copies of older icons and sold their products cheaply to people for whom the icon, even without artistic merit, was nevertheless a holy and deeply revered object. Generally these folk painters clung to the old iconographic schemes and prototypes; but if these were not available, or if the painters sought to put more creative individuality into the work, they painted more freely single groups, garments, and attributes, and even entire incidents from the Bible, with a stronger sense of realism. As a result, figures and compositions were very naïve — "primitive," as we call it in modern art. But for that reason they are the more interesting, because they express the aesthetic feeling of simple people for reality, and they mirror scenes and events from everyday life. Even today many village churches and some of the smaller monasteries are crammed with such naïve folk icons donated in all sincerity by humble believers.

Most icons originating in Bulgaria are rectangular in shape and of dimensions that vary with their purpose. They are constructed of one or two boards glued together, and fastened tightly on the back to prevent buckling. The front side of the older and larger icons is hollowed out in the center, so that the margins form a broad, simple frame roughly half an inch higher than the surface of the image. In later icons this type of framing was abandoned, and replaced by a separate detachable frame ornamented by simple carving in relief. The picture itself was usually painted in tempera on a sized canvas or on wood. Mosaic icons have not been found in Bulgaria, but it cannot be presumed that early examples did not exist since there were mosaic murals in the period of the first and second Bulgarian states. Icons carved in relief are especially rare; they are usually of small dimensions and made of soapstone, ivory, wood, or horn, but there were also large altar icons of marble. Two such icons, with figures in relief depicting the apostles Peter and Paul, date from the late twelfth or early thirteenth century. They were discovered during the excavation of the altar area of the church in the fortress of Tsepena, on the marble iconostasis of which some parts were found. These icons were rectangular slabs about thirty-three inches *110* high, thirteen inches wide, and three inches thick. The apostles, carved in low relief, are standing frontally under an arch supported by columns whose capitals are decorated with an acanthus motif. Paul holds a closed book in his left hand and his other hand rests on his chest, while Peter, in the same pose, clutches his traditional keys in his left hand.[29]

107, 115, 124
129, 99, 127
101, 106, 131
111, 113
140
125, 109, 149

138, 139
103, 154

For the most part, Bulgarian icons faithfully imitate the essential features of old Byzantine prototypes. These were repeated over and over because there was a general dependency on copying; but such celebrated images had, through the centuries, acquired the reputation of possessing miraculous powers, and this was sufficient reason not to change them in any way. Traditionally, the most esteemed icons depicted the Virgin or Christ. For the Virgin, two types enjoyed the greatest favor, the Odegitria and the Eleousa. Christ was most frequently portrayed as the Pantocrator: sometimes He is alone; at other times He is attended by archangels, or by evangelists, prophets, or other saints; He may also appear with the Virgin and John the Baptist, the intercessors for the souls of men, who stretch out their hands imploringly to the Supreme Judge. But there were also pictures of the popular saints: martyrs, saintly warriors, archbishops, hermits, wonder-workers, and others. All of these were depicted according to firmly established traditional types, always in the same garments and with the same attributes, so that the faithful who could not read the identifying inscriptions could nonetheless recognize them. There were icons with mystical subjects such as the Annunciation or the angelic choirs; but there were others with native Bulgarian saints to whom the faithful felt closer, considering these saints to be their special intercessors before God. Whether these icons showed single figures or groups, they were generally painted on a gold background in time-honored poses, in flat and disembodied forms, and in decorative colors. Thus aloof from the earthly world, they moved the faithful as symbols of a higher reality.

135, 151

A favorite subject of the icon painters was the heroic feats of Saints George and Demetrius who accomplish their miraculous deeds astride their horses with magnificently animated gestures. Donors were also portrayed in icons; from Tran there is an example with the Assumption of the Virgin in which, in the lower corner, is the presumed portrait of the donor, a priest who holds in his hand a model of a church.

Icons with scenes from the Gospels were intended for high church holidays and similar occasions. These differed from votive icons because their chief function was to recount or recall the Biblical events, and they often took the place of monumental frescoes in a church. But they also stemmed from a quite different historical and artistic tradition, and their genesis is entirely unrelated either to Hellenistic portraits or to the genre scenes in wall paintings. The representation in icons of Gospel incidents and scenes from the lives of saints are modeled after monumental frescoes in churches, and they faithfully imitate the iconography and style of mural art. However, icon painters did not copy the whole narrative sequence of a fresco but were content to borrow only the principal personages, presenting them in simplified scenes. Thus, in Crucifixions, the walls of Jerusalem are only sketched in to define the place where the event occurred. Even though the Gospels describe many other participants, the icons show only the Virgin and Saint John standing on either side of the Cross as sole witnesses to Christ's sacrifice.

Often the Bulgarian icon painters of the sixteenth and seventeenth centuries strive with their modest means to express their own stylistic conceptions and sense of composition and to modify either the scenes as a whole or certain traditional details. On these icons intended for the great church feasts, the action is usually set in crowded mountainous landscapes, or in front of an architectural background that may be reduced to schematically painted watchtowers and crenelated battlements. Outdoor settings are strongly simplified into two stylized mountain peaks at left

153

and right with the sparsest of vegetation. On an icon of the Transfiguration of Christ, these two mountains are represented as two parallel white streams, like the rivers in paintings of the Baptism. The trees are particularly scanty and simplified and the figures, resembling ponderous old men,

L

display conventional postures, neither standing nor lying on the ground. What is exceptional in this icon is the background: two horizontal planes are laid out one above the other, a grayish blue sky beneath a gold heaven. In an icon of the Raising of Lazarus, however, the artist reveals *145* a feeling for space; the panel is crammed with mountains, buildings, and a number of figures, all distributed on five different levels. Particularly interesting is the attempt to convey the widespread area of Jerusalem, bounded by two of its watchtowers.

Nowhere does a Bulgarian icon painter show a more free and easy attitude toward the iconographic tradition than in the icon of Saint Ivan of Rila. It evidently owes little to old iconographic *154* formulas; instead it takes its images from the saint's biography or, better, from the oral tradition that still survives today in his birthplace. True, there are the two conventional mountains; the saint is also presented in a frontal pose in his monk's cowl with his martyr's cross in one hand and an open scroll in the other, as he is on the fresco in the Church of Saints Peter and Paul in Tirnovo. But all the other details — Saint Ivan as a lad in the cave on Mount Ruen, the two deer in the lower right corner, and the pine tree on the left-hand mountain — are apparently motifs borrowed from folklore. Precisely because of these details, this icon seems to be a product of folk art rather than a votive or festival icon. Like all other Bulgarian icon painters of the seventeenth and eighteenth centuries, its author was not acquainted with the theory of perspective during the Renaissance, or with the naturalism and sculptural modeling of Western painting in that period. Neither were Bulgarian artists influenced by the Italo-Greek school of icon painting that was famous in those centuries. The relationship of the human figures to architectural and natural forms is unreal; the coloring of objects and landscapes is equally unnatural, which in no way detracts from the decorative effect of the whole. It is clear that this approach was not accidental but the result of a deliberate aim, and achieved by the expressive exploitation of an extremely limited range of colors.

During the dark years of political and religious oppression, the folk-style icon painters strayed from the traditional iconographic formulas to find a more personal expression to accompany new aesthetic conceptions. This led to the first attempts to create a folk art, though its subject matter did not usually extend beyond the limits of the well-defined realm of religious ideas. On the raised flat frames of many icons were painted individual figures of prophets, apostles, and *131* evangelists — holy personages who have some ideal relationship to the chief subject of the icon. Icons that have scenes on their frames from the lives, miracles, and martyrdoms of saints are *115, 117, 119* far from rare. Many such scenes resemble miniature paintings and could be considered genuine *130, 141* genre compositions. On an icon reproduced here, the artist painted on the frame not only the *140* evangelists and apostles, but also the popular Bulgarian saints Joachim Osogovski, Gabriel Lesnovski, Hilarion Meglenski, and Prohor Pčinjski.

Of particular interest are icons with silver or gilded casings which conceal the entire background and often even the bodies of the figures, leaving only the faces exposed. These are generally large icons, intended for an iconostasis given in homage to the church by prominent donors and benefactors. The metal covers are ornamented with stylized geometrical or floral motifs, or even reli- *106* gious emblems and figures of saints, all embossed in low relief. An exception is the icon from *107* 1342, mentioned above, which was presented as a gift to the Monastery of the Virgin Eleousa in Nessebri. Parts of its original casing were replaced in the seventeenth century by a new casing, but the rest constitutes a real rarity among icons in the Balkan peninsula; the icon case itself was used as a donation charter, a formal deed recording the gift of the icon. The background was overlaid with gilded silver leaf on which, in place of the usual embossed ornamental motifs, there are three lengthy inscriptions: these tell of the Bulgarian ruler under whom the gift was made; of when and by whom the monastery church was renovated; and of the gifts presented to the church at that time. In this commemorative inscription the donor of the icon is not mentioned by name, but the "anonymous" benefactor could not resist the temptation of perpetuating his identity: cleverly concealed on the small enameled plaques enframing the Virgin's face can be made out the words, "During the reign of Alexander and Michael Asen, their great-uncle Samuel ...offered this garland."[30]

Icons could be found everywhere in Bulgaria, not only in churches but also in private dwellings. In churches, they covered the area between the pillars of the iconostasis which separated the congregation from the altar itself. These icons were large-scale images of the Virgin, Christ, and John the Baptist, and of the patron saint of the particular church and other saints as well. The icons of Christ and the Virgin were always placed on either side of the middle doors, the so-called

144 Imperial Doors, over which always hung an Annunciation with the Archangel Gabriel and Mary. In the seventeenth and eighteenth centuries, when the iconostasis became a more complex architectural structure of two or even three stories, the number of tiers of icons increased. The carved iconostasis became an imposing wall covered with large icons grouped according to their subjects, with those in the center pertaining to the Last Judgment. Above the large icons, the spaces between pillars were filled with smaller ones; in this tier, the icon of Christ occupied the center, flanked by those of the Virgin and John the Baptist, always shown in prayerful supplication as the intercessors for the souls of men before the Pantocrator. These three icons constituted the well-known composition called the Deësis, which also often appears as a single icon containing the three figures. To either side of the Deësis are icons with half-length figures of angels and the twelve apostles. When the iconostasis has a third tier, the icons on that level illustrate the incidents from the Gospels that are celebrated in the twelve chief feasts of the Orthodox Church, themselves

148 symbolic of the twelve basic Christian dogmas. In the middle of that tier the Crucifix is placed, with Christ painted on a gilded wooden cross; on either side are icons of the Virgin and Saint John the Evangelist, in the same mournful poses that they have in larger compositions of the Crucifixion scene.

Similar to these large altar icons were others which were carried around outside the church in solemn processions and liturgical functions. Some of these are double-sided, and among their subjects are Christ, the Virgin and Child, and the Crucifixion. Such icons were used in Bulgaria only up to the end of the fourteenth century because, under Turkish rule, liturgical functions were only permitted inside the churches. In the so-called Tomitch Psalter from the fourteenth century, now in the Historical Museum, Moscow, there are two miniatures which show liturgical functions celebrated in front of icons of this type. In one miniature, a large icon of Christ Pantocrator occupies the center, set up on a tripod and covered by a red cloth with a gold cross on it. The upper part of the icon is concealed by a white cloth whose ends hang down beneath the icon. On either side, candles burn in tall gold candlesticks. At the right of the icon there are four priests standing in white robes with hands upraised in prayer, three singers, and a youth in red dressed in aristocratic fashion.

The central position in the other miniature is taken by an icon of the Odegitria Virgin; it is draped in the same fashion as in the first miniature, and flanked on either side by priests in white robes and hoods, behind whom are two secular personages, and to the right is a group of four singers. All of these figures raise their hands in prayer before the icon. In both miniatures there is a grassy plot of ground with flowers, proof that the artist's aim was to depict a liturgical service taking place out-of-doors in the presence of lay persons. The publisher of the miniatures in the Tomitch Psalter maintains that they are a true reflection of Bulgarian life in the fourteenth century, and this is surely the case.[31]

The Orthodox Church tolerates the practice of the kissing of icons as an expression of veneration for Christ, the Virgin, and the saints. This custom, as we quoted above, was mentioned as early as the tenth century by Presbyter Cosmas, an ardent champion of icon worship. It continued into the seventeenth and eighteenth centuries, even after new multistoried iconostases put the upper tiers of icons out of reach of the faithful; portable icons of smaller dimensions were introduced, often with double faces, and placed low in front of the altar. For feasts in celebration of some particular event in the Gospels, or of some saint, the appropriate icon was set up on a special pedestal, the proskynetarion.

Icons used in private dwellings were similar in appearance to the portable icons in churches. They were hung on the east wall or in a corner of the room, either on small iconostases or directly on the bare wall. There they were venerated as earnestly as the more imposing images in the churches. These domestic icons were often made up of two or three panels, constituting diptychs or triptychs.

Especially interesting and particularly typical of Bulgaria, although they are rare even there, are what may be called didactic icons. These first appeared in the early seventeenth century and were designed to turn men's thoughts to more virtuous conduct and the performance of worthwhile acts. They showed how to participate in church services and how to take communion and make full confession, as well as warning against indulging in drink and consorting with sorcerers and witches. Didactic icons were generally products of folk art and are characteristically naïve in composition. In the eighteenth and nineteenth centuries, such scenes and illustrations of Bible episodes were often painted on the entrance walls of churches as well.

Thus it can be seen that the Bulgarian icons, of which a representative selection is reproduced in these pages, mirror the chief events of the thousand years of their history. The development of icon painting was closely linked not only with that of painting in its larger forms, but also with Bulgarian life from the ninth to the nineteenth century. Throughout that vast span of time the icon was a religious object, indispensable to the Orthodox liturgy, and an important element in social and domestic life. Its initial appearance in Bulgaria and its historical significance in that country nevertheless transcend the narrow boundaries of a single nation and its political fortunes.

Notes, Part III

1 G. I. KACAROV and H. TASCHEV, A Newly Discovered Early Christian Tomb in Sofia, Bulletin of the Bulgarian Archeological Institute, I, 1910, pp. 23 ff. (in Bulgarian). KR. MIATEV, Decorative Painting in the Necropolis of Sofia, Sofia, 1925, p. 96 (in Bulgarian)

2 A. GRABAR, La Peinture religieuse en Bulgarie, Paris, 1928, pp. 26, 45 ff.

3 KP. МИЯТЕВ, Преславската керамика, Sofia, 1936 (KR. MIATEV, The Ceramics of Preslav); idem, The Rotunda in Preslav, Sofia, 1932, pp. 113 ff.

4 KR. MIATEV, Two Fragments in the Poem of the Exarch John as a Historical Source, Archeology, I, 1959, 1-2, 9-16 (in Bulgarian)

5 EMIL GEORGIEV, The Flowering of Bulgarian Literature in the IXth and Xth Centuries, Sofia, 1962, pp. 219 ff. (in Bulgarian)

6 M. G. POPRUŽENKO, The Presbyter Kosmas, a Bulgarian Author of the Xth Century, Sofia, 1936 (in Bulgarian). The passages cited here are taken from the polemics against the Bogomils according to Popruženko's edition, pp. 488, 502, 503, 504, 545

7 Greek Sources of Bulgarian History, V, p. 274

8 KR. MIATEV, The Ceramics of Preslav, pp. 13 ff., ill. 2

9 IV. DUITSCHEV, The Rebellion under Ases and the Cult of St. Demetrius of Thessalonica, Collected Works of the Bulgarian Academy of Art and Science, XI, 1949, p. 51 (in Bulgarian)

10 A. GRABAR, The Church Tomb in the Cloister of Bačkovo, Bulletin of the Bulgarian Archeological Institute, II, 1923-1924, pp. 11 ff. (in Bulgarian); idem, La Peinture religieuse en Bulgarie, pp. 57 ff. Such imitations of icons are found also elsewhere than in Bulgaria: Church of Saint Barbara, Soganle (Cappadocia); Church of Saint Sophia, Kiev; Nerezi; Žiča

11 A. GRABAR, La Peinture religieuse, Paris, 1928, p. 104

12 A. GRABAR, La Peinture religieuse, Paris, 1928, p.126; KR. MIATEV, Die Fresken aus Bojana, Sofia-Dresden, 1961, p. 12

13 A. GRABAR, The Church Tomb in the Cloister of Bačkovo, p. 57

14 M. КОВАЧЕВ, Драгалевският манастир Св. Богородица Витошка, Sofia, 1940 (M. KOVATSCHEV, The Cloister of the Virgin of Vitoša in Dragalevo), pp. 134 ff., ill. 39

15 A. GRABAR, La Peinture religieuse, Paris, 1928, p. 120; KR. MIATEV, Die Fresken aus Bojana, p. 11

16 A. GRABAR, La Peinture religieuse, Paris, 1928, p. 251

17 A. GRABAR, La Peinture religieuse, Paris, 1928, p. 251

18 A. GRABAR, La Peinture religieuse, Paris, 1928, p. 328

19 M. КОВАЧЕВ, Драгалевският манастир Св. Богородица Витошка, Sofia, 1940 (M. KOVATSCHEV, The Cloister of the Virgin of Vitoša in Dragalevo), pp. 127 ff., ills. 95-98

20 A. GRABAR, La Peinture religieuse, Paris, 1928, p. 327. The standard given to the Monastery of Zographos by Stephen the Great in 1500 is apparently a copy of this icon

21 A. GRABAR, Нерукотвореный Спас Ланского Собора. Prague, 1930, p. 9 (in Russian); KR. MIATEV, On the Origin of the Icon "La Sainte Face de Laon," Belgrade, 1964

22 Н. П. КОНДАКОВ, Русская икона, I, Prague, 1931 (N. P. KONDAKOV, Russian Icons), p. 87

23 КР. МИЯТЕВ, Към иконографията на Богородица Умиление, Известия на Българския археологически институт, III, Sofia, 1925 (KR. MIATEV, On the Iconography of the Virgin Eleousa, Bulletin of the Bulgarian Archeological Institute), p. 160, pl. III

24 I. VELKOV, La Basilique de la mer à Messemvrie, Recueil Uspenskij I, Paris, 1930, p. 78, pl. I

25 T. GERASIMOV, L'Icône bilatérale de Poganovo, Cahiers archéologiques X, 1959, pp. 279-288; A. GRABAR, A propos d'une icône byzantine du XIVe siècle au Musée de Sofia, Cahiers archéologiques, X, pp. 289-304

26 Exh. cat., L'Art Byzantin — Art Européen, Athens, 1964, p. 247

27 КР. МИЯТЕВ, Към иконографията на Богородица Умиление, Известия на Блгарскияъ археологически институт, III, Sofia, 1925 (KR. MIATEV, On the Iconography of the Virgin Eleousa, Bulletin of the Bulgarian Archeological Institute), pp. 171 ff.

28 PAISKI HILENDARSKI, Slavic-Bulgarian History, Sofia, 1963, p. 93

29 P. SIRKU, Die alte Čepiner Festung im Dorfe Dorkovo und zwei byzantinische Reliefs aus Čepina, Byzantinische Zeitschrift, V, 1898, Heft 4, pp. 612, 842, Taf. III (in Bulgarian)

30 T. ГЕРАСИМОВ, Новооткрит надпис върху иконата Богородица Умиление от Несебър, Известия на Народния музей в Бургас, I, Burgas, 1950 (T. GERASIMOV, A Newly Discovered Inscription on the Icon of the Virgin Eleousa from Nesebar, Bulletin of the National Museum, Burgas), pp. 253-256, pls. XVII, XVIII

31 M. V. CEPKINA, Bulgarian Miniatures of the XIVth Century, Moscow, 1963, pp. 72, 82, 154, pls. 41, 63 (in Russian)

97 SAINT THEODORE. Late 9th-early 10th centuries. Fragment of a glazed ceramic icon. $21^7/_8 \times 17^3/_8''$. Archaeological Museum, Preslav

99 OUR LADY OF MERCY (ELEOUSA VIRGIN). 13th-14th centuries. Double-faced icon (see plate 101). $49^1/_4 \times 38^5/_8''$. Archaeological Museum, Sofia

101 CHRIST PANTOCRATOR. 13th-14th centuries. Double-faced icon (see plate 99). $49^1/_4 \times 38^5/_8''$. Archaeological Museum, Sofia

102 VIRGIN OF KATAFIGI. Detail, plate 103

103 VIRGIN OF KATAFIGI AND SAINT JOHN THE EVANGELIST. c. 1395. Double-faced icon (see plate 105). $35 \times 23^5/_8''$. Archaeological Museum, Sofia

105 MIRACLE IN THE MONASTERY OF CHRIST LATOM. c. 1395. Double-faced icon (see plate 103). $35 \times 23^5/_8''$. Archaeological Museum, Sofia

106 CHRIST PANTOCRATOR. 14th century. $47^1/_4 \times 32^1/_4''$. Archaeological Museum, Sofia

107 ODEGITRIA VIRGIN. 1342. $51^1/_8 \times 42^1/_8''$. Archaeological Museum, Sofia

108 SAINT IVAN OF RILA. 14th century. $30^3/_4 \times 21^5/_8''$. State Museum, Monastery of Rila

109 THE APOSTLE ANDREW. 15th century. Double-faced icon. $12^5/_8 \times 10^1/_4''$. Church Museum, Sofia

110 SAINTS GEORGE AND DEMETRIUS ON HORSEBACK. 14th-15th centuries. Icon in relief. Dimensions with frame, $33^1/_2 \times 31^1/_2''$; without frame, $11^3/_8 \times 11^3/_8''$. Church Museum, Sofia

111 CHRIST THE KING OF KINGS WITH THE VIRGIN AND SAINT JOHN THE BAPTIST. 16th century. $50^3/_4 \times 43^1/_4''$. National Art Gallery, Sofia

112 VIRGIN. Detail, plate 113

113 CHRIST ENTHRONED WITH THE VIRGIN AND SAINT JOHN THE BAPTIST. 1497. $42^1/_2 \times 28^3/_4''$. Monastery of Bačkovo

115 ODEGITRIA or KEHARITOMENE VIRGIN. 16th century. Double-faced icon (see plate 121). $42^1/_8 \times 32^5/_8''$. Church Museum, Sofia

117 BIRTH OF THE VIRGIN. Detail, plate 115

119 MEETING OF JOACHIM AND ANNE AT THE GOLDEN GATE. Detail, plate 115

120 SAINT JOHN THE EVANGELIST AT THE CROSS. Detail, plate 121

121 CRUCIFIXION. 16th century. Double-faced icon (see plate 115). $42^1/_8 \times 32^5/_8''$. Church Museum, Sofia

122 CRUCIFIXION. 1541. Double-faced icon (see plate 124). $41^3/_8 \times 28^3/_8''$. Church Museum, Sofia

123 SAINT JOHN THE EVANGELIST AT THE CROSS. Detail, plate 122

124 ODEGITRIA or PHANEROMENE VIRGIN. 1541. Double-faced icon (see plate 122). $41^3/_8 \times 28^3/_8''$. Church Museum, Sofia

125 SAINT GEORGE ENTHRONED. 16th century. $31^1/_2 \times 21^1/_8''$. National Art Gallery, Plovdiv

127 ELEOUSA VIRGIN. 17th century. $11^1/_2 \times 9^1/_2''$. Monastery of Bačkovo.

129 VIRGIN AND CHILD. 16th century. $50^3/_8 \times 33^1/_2''$. National Art Gallery, Plovdiv

130 SAINT JOHN THE BAPTIST AND SCENES FROM HIS LIFE. 1694. $36^3/_4 \times 25^5/_8''$. Archaeological Museum, Sofia

131 CHRIST PANTOCRATOR ENTHRONED. 1642. $30^3/_8 \times 20^7/_8''$. Church Museum, Sofia

132 ENTRY INTO JERUSALEM. 17th century. 15×8¹/₈″. Church Museum, Sofia

133 HOSPITALITY OF ABRAHAM (OLD TESTAMENT TRINITY). 1652. Signed Nedelko the Painter. 36⁵/₈×27¹/₂″. Church Museum, Sofia

135 SAINT GEORGE AND THE DRAGON. 1667. Signed Vassili the Monk. 34⁵/₈×24³/₄″. National Art Gallery, Sofia

137 DIDACTIC ICON. 1620. 41³/₈×30³/₈″. Monastery of Dragalevci

138 TWO ANGELS. Detail, plate 139

139 COUNCIL OF THE ARCHANGEL MICHAEL AND OTHER ANGELIC POWERS. 17th century. 42¹/₈×24³/₄″. Monastery of Bačkovo

140 CHRIST PANTOCRATOR. 17th century. 35³/₈×26″. Monastery of the Holy Trinity, Etropole

141 SAINT JOHN THE BAPTIST. 17th century. 35×24³/₄″. National Art Gallery, Sofia

142 BAPTISM OF CHRIST. 17th century. 19⁵/₈×13³/₈″. Church Museum, Sofia

143 THREE ANGELS. Detail, plate 142.

144 ANNUNCIATION. 17th century. The Imperial doors from an iconostasis. Dimensions of both panels together, 54³/₈×30⁷/₈″. National Art Gallery, Sofia

145 RAISING OF LAZARUS. 17th century. 13×9¹/₄″. Archaeological Museum, Sofia

146 BAPTISM OF CHRIST. 17th century. 13×9¹/₄″. Archaeological Museum, Sofia

147 THE FORTY MARTYRS. 1780. 16¹/₈×13¹/₄″. National Art Gallery, Sofia

148 VIRGIN. 17th century. One of a group of three icons depicting the Crucifixion on an iconostasis. 16¹/₂×7¹/₂″. Monastery of Bačkovo

149 SAINT MARINA. 17th century. 24³/₈×11″. Church Museum, Sofia

151 SAINTS GEORGE AND DEMETRIUS ON HORSEBACK. 17th century. Portion of a frieze from an iconostasis. 28³/₄×35″. Church Museum, Sofia

153 TRANSFIGURATION. 18th century. 13¹/₄×9⁷/₈″. Archaeological Museum, Sofia

154 SAINT IVAN OF RILA. 17th century. 12×9¹/₂″. Archaeological Museum, Sofia

155 NATIVITY. 18th century. 14×9⁵/₈″. Archaeological Museum, Sofia

156 NATIVITY. 17th-18th centuries. 15³/₄×7⁷/₈″. Monastery of Bačkovo

ΘΥ ΠΡ

ΓΟΡΓΩ

99

102

107

СТ҃Ы   ІꙎЗ

РАДЧ   АНЬ

108

IC ΧC

Ο ΩΝ

MP ΘΥ ΟΜΕΓ

 Α̅ Χ̅ Ρ̅ΔΣ

Ο ΑΓΙ Ω ΙΩ Ο ΠΡΟ

111

113

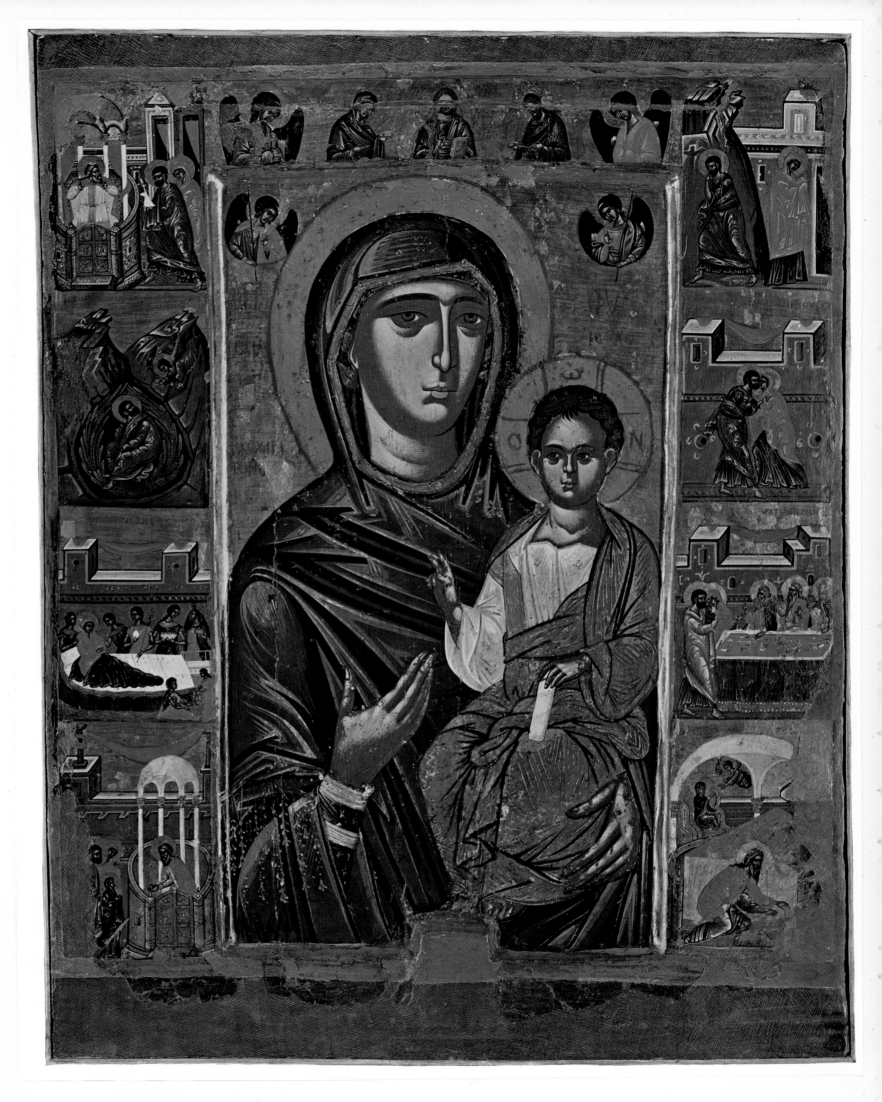

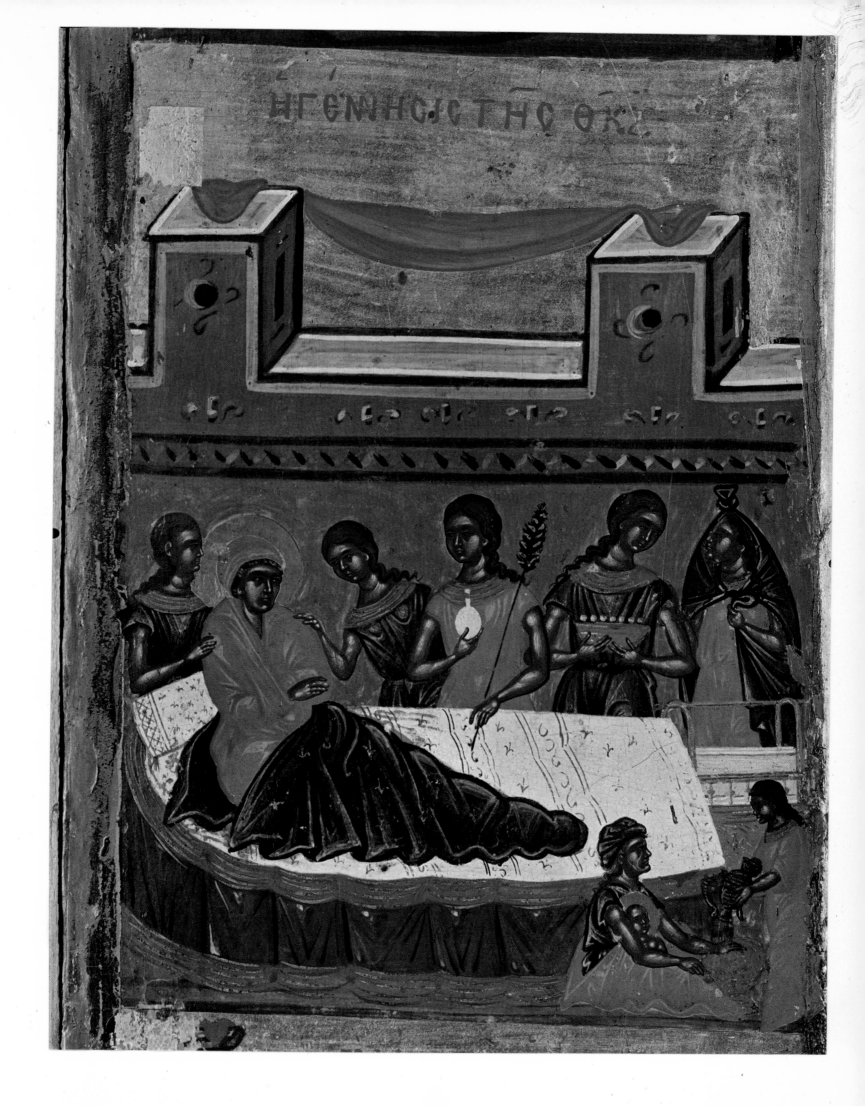

119

124

127

129

130